cars in films

First published in October 2002

A catalogue record for this book is available from the British Library

ISBN 1 85960 682 2

Library of Congress catalog card no. 00135911

Published by Haynes Publishing, Sparkford, Yeovil, Somerset BA22 7JJ, England

Tel: 01963 442030 Fax: 01963 440001
Int. tel: +44 1963 442030 Int. fax: +44 1963 440001
E-mail: sales@haynes-manuals.co.uk
Website: www.haynes.co.uk

Haynes North America, Inc.,
861 Lawrence Drive, Newbury Park,
California 91320, USA

Designed by Simon Larkin

Printed and bound in England by J. H. Haynes & Co. Ltd, Sparkford

Front cover main image: *Bullitt* (Warner/Solar/BFI)

martin buckley with andrew roberts

cars in films

great moments from post-war international cinema

contents

introduction

CAR SPOTTING IN FILMS is a skill I acquired many years ago, nurtured from the late '70s on a diet of late night TV. Cars, especially old cars, were my obsession and I found I could feed my habit with a flow of rare and exotic machinery mainlined from a small black-and-white portable television.

I say 'skill' because I became an expert at recognising cars merely from the shape of an inside window frame, a roof or a shadowy outline, or even the sound of an engine (often overdubbed). Cars parked casually in the street could sometimes be more important than those driven by the actors. In location-shot films, the background to street scenes offered snapshots of automotive life as it really was in the '50s, '60s and early '70s.

I learned to watch films on two levels, my attention split between the main story line and the movements of the true (automotive) stars as they slipped in and out of the narrative.

In most films the cars are just props: four-wheeled extras that cruise past a closed set to give an appearance of period reality. The trained eye can spot the same car going past several times in a single scene, and just occasionally I would see the same cars pop up as background extras in different films. Period recreations, on the other hand, became almost unbearable to watch because of the blunders: usually involving cars that hadn't even been introduced in the year the film is supposed to be set. It's one thing to believe that a chance encounter may lead, as so often in the movies, to a whirlwind romance or a web of espionage, but a Ford Cortina MkII in 1961? That would be suspending disbelief from too great a height.

The critics' verdict on a particular film became of only passing interest to me as I developed a feel for the kind of films that would yield the best car sightings. Dubbed-over Euro-gangster films of the early '70s (the ones where everybody speaks out of sync in the same gravelly mid-Atlantic accent) were good for rare gems, while Jaguars, police Wolseleys and Austin Westminsters featured heavily in any British film with a crime theme. These were mock-ups, I learned later, hired out by companies that specialised in police vehicles for film work in the '60s and '70s. Look closely and you'll see not only the same number plates appearing time after time but also the same fake-uniformed stunt men driving the cars in dozens of different films.

In American films I never knew quite what I was going to get. There was lots of Detroit stuff, of course – and a strong feel for the product placement that was going on even then – but also a wide variety of the European cars that were imported into North America. *Annie Hall's* VW Beetle was totally predictable, but seeing a Skoda Octavia in *North By Northwest* always comes as a bit of a surprise. The same principle applies to Australian films, whose backgrounds offered a fascinating blend of American cars, locally-built British hybrids such as the Austin Lancers in *They're A Weird Mob* and, by the 1970s, Isuzu Belletts, Nissan Cedrics and other Japanese wonders barely known in the UK.

Certain cars became metaphors for the characters who were driving them on screen. There was a period in the late '70s and early '80s when the 'interesting' liberal, left-wing hero or heroine of Hollywood films – typically a 'crusading' journalist – would always drive a rusty BMW 2002, a Beetle, a DS Safari or an early Ford Mustang to prove that he/she was not a tool of corporate marketing. The classic case was perhaps Robert Redford, as Bob Woodward in *All the President's Men*, uncovering the Watergate scandal in his down-at-heel but dogged Volvo Amazon. In the Watergate-Vietnam years it was easy to see the lavish products of Motor City as symbols of an ugly and bloated system.

However, it seems that Hollywood sees something questionable about American men with European cars, and Jags and Italian cars especially were used in films as signs of dangerous over-sophistication and questionable sexuality from as early as the 1940s. In *Play Misty for Me* even Clint Eastwood falls foul of a psychotic woman, presumably as a comeuppance for his flagrant self-indulgence in choosing to drive an XK150. Old-fashioned American cars began their comeback about the time of *The Deer Hunter*, in which Robert de Niro's tailfin Cadillac shows that he at least is one man who holds on to American patriotism, even after the fall of Saigon.

Meanwhile, a high-powered international villain, as like as not, would be chauffeured around in a Mercedes 600 with heavily tinted windows; FBI agents seemed always to drive suspiciously innocuous blue Ford sedans bereft of their hubcaps; and spivs and gangsters in 1950s British crime films used either dated Canadian imports or MkVII Jaguars.

I also began to get a feel for the cars that weren't going to make it through a particular film, like those horror fans who always know which character will be the first victim. In the crime genre, anything more than 10 years older than the date of the picture usually ended up either ablaze or smashed to bits, and for the car fan like me this could be painful to see. I know people who cannot watch *Get Carter* without shedding a tear for the white Sunbeam Alpine that disappears into the murky waters of the Tyne harbour. To them, the girl trapped in the boot is neither here nor there.

As my knowledge grew I naturally acquired a taste for ever more obscure 'sightings', and I found the most remarkable cars in the most unlikely places: Laurence Harvey driving off in a Maserati Quattroporte in the closing moments of *Life at the Top* or piloting a cream 300d 'Adenaur' in *Butterfield 8*; a Lamborghini Islero in *The Man Who Haunted Himself* and a BMW 2000CS in *The Brain*. All of the above was churning over in my brain for years, to be given an airing only when I recognised a fellow sufferer: favourite car chases is still not acceptable dinner party conversation as far as I know. Yet I began to sense that I was not alone, as the films and cars that had excited me on my little black-and-white portable all those years ago began to acquire a cult following.

Cars in Films sounds like a horrifyingly big subject, but I've honed it down to the essence of what people like me find exciting about it, and it's probably easier to tell you what is out rather than what is in. It is not intended to be an exhaustive A to Z reference guide to the car in films from day one. Cars and cinema have been around so long now that any such book would be the size of two London telephone directories, probably just about as digestible and beyond my historical range. Film-makers were quick to see the dramatic possibilities of the automobile in their flickering, soundless creations at the beginning of the last century but you'll forgive me if I leave it for another book – and another author – to tell you about the Keystone Cops and their Model-T Fords or the chases in nearly every George Formby comedy. I'm never happy writing on subjects that don't have any relevance for me.

Even in terms of post-war cinema this is more of a personal selection, governed by my own eccentric viewing and also by what archives had to offer in terms of relevant stills. In many cases the stills photographer didn't bother to take a picture of the car in question, which is hardly surprising in the case of low-budget films for which publicity stills were a dispensable luxury and certainly weren't going to be wasted on what was seen as an inanimate bit part player. Neither is colour material as plentiful as I had hoped: I've learned that as late as the 1980s stills photography was in black-and-white even for colour movies (again, a matter of cost). Posters, on the other hand, are almost always in colour and give an excellent period flavour and examples are included wherever possible. Although not pretending to be a complete guide the book is certainly not a mere coffee-table glossy, and I hope I have pitched it at a level that will satisfy a wide range of readers.

It is post-war cars and post-war films that, for me, have all the resonance and push all the right style and imagery buttons. Post-war film-makers learned how to make cars look sexy on screen, conveying their speed, their dynamism and their danger, thanks to better cameras, better film and better sound. It is a skill that peaked somewhere in the '60s, with the James Bond films in the vanguard. *Goldfinger* and that silver Aston Martin set a standard for the Bond series that has yet to be bettered. Here, for the first time, was the motor car as a sexy piece of high-tech hardware, definitively

The fiery end of the supposed Dodge Challenger after it hit the shovels of the road-block bulldozers at speed in *Vanishing Point*. Look closely and you'll see it's actually a Chevrolet Camaro. *(Photo: TCF/Cupid (Norman Spencer)/Pictorial Press Limited)*

Yves Montand at the wheel of this Renault lorry with its explosive load of nitroglycerine in the tense 1953 film *The Wages of Fear*. *(Photo: Film Sonar/Cicc-Vera/ Pictorial Press Limited)*

The 'droogs' from Stanley Kubrick's 1971 film *A Clockwork Orange* aboard their Marcos Mantis prototype. The car still exists. *(Photo: Warner/Polaris/ Pictorial Press Limited)*

moving the films away from Fleming's Bentley-driving hero and delivering a performance as memorable as the character himself.

Beyond Bond there has been a rash of stylishly choreographed chase sequences featuring more realistic male heroes whose ambiguous social status threw their cars into sharper relief. The films became set piece '60s classics, a genre epitomised by the likes of *Bullitt* and *The Italian Job*. Now, if your religion is cars, then these two films are like visual tracts from an automobile bible, to be dutifully viewed at any opportunity. Their enduring appeal lies not only in the way they celebrated the motor car when, for me, it was at its most potently stylish, but also in the way that they captured the Zeitgeist of the period. Viewed from a distance of 30 years the cars, the clothes, the sound tracks and the stars – the brooding machismo of McQueen and the cheeky cockney appeal of Michael Caine at his best – seem cooler than ever. I'm part of a generation that only ever saw these films on television when they were already a decade old.

But I'm also part of the generation that saw the video recorder become an affordable domestic appliance. Suddenly I was able to re-live my favourite *Italian Job* moments again and again. I could record them off the telly and take them apart frame by frame with the pause button or, with the volume turned up to maximum, attain a transcendental state as the 13-minute chase sequence in *Bullitt* built up to its tyre-squealing climax. If you recognise these disturbing symptoms then this is the book for you.

So, on the basis of the above, is *Cars in Films* a book exclusively for sad post-war petrol heads? Well, not entirely. Certainly you'll find *Le Mans*, *Grand Prix*, a sprinkling of the teenage exploitation hotrod B-movies and all the classic stunts, races and chases from *The Blue Lamp* to *Ronin* within its pages. Yet it gives equal weight to all kinds of other films where cars merely set the scene or say something about a time, a place or a character. It is a book for unreconstructed car freaks, to be sure, but also a book for those who can get as excited about James Fox and his

white Mk2 Jaguar in *Performance* (probably my favourite film ever) or the Ford GT40 in *Un Homme et Une Femme* as they can about the muscle cars and hot-rods in *Two-Lane Blacktop* or *American Graffiti*. In this way I hope that *Cars in Films* sets itself apart from previous books on the subject.

The breadth of cars featured should satisfy most tastes. From '60s Grand Prix cars to hot-rods, from obscure exotica to period saloons. There's a wide range of human stars too, though mostly men it has to be said. Terry-Thomas in a thinly disguised Aston Martin DB3S, George C. Scott in a BMW 503 and Burt Reynolds in a Citroën SM.

There are films here you had forgotten about and some you never knew existed. There might even be, come to think of it, a few cars you'd forgotten existed – like the Crayford Mini convertible from *Night Must Fall* or the futuristic Marcos Mantis prototype used in *A Clockwork Orange*. Strictly speaking, only cars are covered, but I've allowed a few exceptions to slip in where the film is sufficiently evocative. You'll see Stanley Baker and the Austin tipper trucks in *Hell Drivers*, Yves Montand and the Renault lorries in *The Wages of Fear*, the Kenworth juggernaut in *Duel*, Steve McQueen's dune buggy in *The Thomas Crown Affair*.

If the overall content has no particular rationale, then at least the chapters seem to form quite naturally and, what's more, some interesting trends emerge. Car themes figure disproportionately heavily in comedy films from *Genevieve* through to *Monte Carlo or Bust*, *The Great Race* and the *Herbie* series, before tailing off in the '70s into self-indulgent dross like *The Cannonball Run* and *Gumball Rally*. Road movies form a definite group, although, with a couple of notable exceptions, the genre only seems to work when set in the context of the wide-open spaces of North America. Inspired by the hippy ethos of *Easy Rider*, they hit their peak at the turn of the '70s with *Vanishing Point* and the lesser *Dirty Mary Crazy Larry*, and have popped up again regularly ever since, most memorably, perhaps, in *Thelma and Louise*.

The crime film opens up a rich vein of material, including

great films like *Robbery* (featuring the second best car chase ever filmed), *Get Carter* and *Villain* where large lumbering saloons driven by men in stocking masks meet violent ends. Such films, which brought a new kind of hardbitten realism to the British cops and robbers flick, were the inspiration for *The Sweeney* TV series which, in turn, produced a couple of cinema release spin-offs in the same violent mould – the imaginatively titled *Sweeney!* and *Sweeney 2*. Even John Wayne left his horse behind to make a couple of reasonable action thrillers in the early '70s. *McQ* seems to have been inspired by *Dirty Harry* and the four-wheeled headcount includes the trashing of a brand new Pontiac Firebird. In *Brannigan*, set in London, Wayne – complete with paunch and hairpiece – leaps Tower Bridge and lands a new Ford Capri in a skip.

I've grouped horror and fantasy together. *Death Race 2000* sits happily enough with films like *The Car* and *Christine*. A personal favourite is *The Devil Rides Out*, set in the '20s and featuring the wonderful Charles Gray and a dice between a Lancia Lambda and a 3-litre Bentley.

Heroes and Villains is a catch-all title that embraces some meaty stuff. Cary Grant, Grace Kelly and a Sunbeam Alpine in *To Catch a Thief*; Paul Newman and a '58 Cadillac Biarritz in *Hud*, James Dean and a custom Mercury in *Rebel Without a Cause*. *The Godfather* films have featured some impeccable period cars, like the Touring bodied Alfa Romeo that gets blown up in the original 1973 film.

The James Bond films form a major section of the Spies and Espionage chapter, though the astronomical cost of reproductions alone means that this must be a personal snapshot rather than a definitive guide. The spoof Bonds often drove serious cars: James Coburn an Excalibur in *Our Man Flint*, for instance, John Phillip Law twin E-types in *Diabolik*, and Peter Sellers in *Casino Royale* was exposed to cars whose heartbreaking beauty can only have quickened the breakdown that sabotaged that film with more devastating effect than any Bond villain has brought to bear on Messrs Connery, Moore *et al*.

I have made it a point of principle that no film has earned a place in this book through dramatic merit or entertainment value. Any merit over and above car interest is a bonus. It's a reasonable rule of thumb that any film with cars as a central theme is an almost guaranteed turkey. When the theme is motorsport the casualty rate surges up to near 100%. *Checkpoint*, *The Green Helmet*, *Le Mans* and *Redline 7000* featured some fabulous cars against a background of enough wooden acting to rebuild every Morris Traveller ever made. Never was the fast-forward button so useful.

Some cars on film can travel in time as well as space. The superficially innocuous Wolseleys, Rileys and Morrises of Ealing and post-Ealing films transport us to a wondrous fantasy-Britain of litter-free streets, functioning trains, decent coppers and chaps saying 'gosh' every so often. Some evoke a past era brilliantly – the automotive research evident in *Newsfront* is superb. Others, more amusingly, create a space-time conjunction that Captain Kirk could never have found. The low-budget *Quadrophenia* is set in 1965 but has scrapheaps of '70s cars and *Star Wars* showing in cinemas. With a bigger budget and less excuse *The Dirty Dozen: The Next Mission* has 1979-model London taxis, and *Escape to Athena*, another Second World War epic, features Fiat 1100Rs whose drivers have collar-length hair.

The film scholar Andrew Roberts, who spends far too much time in darkened rooms in front of a VCR, has been of invaluable assistance in the preparation of this book. His knowledge of films and his ability to analyse them with intelligence and wit is only matched by his knowledge of cars. He is really the joint author and also helped locate and secure a great number of the images used here. I should also extend my thanks to Bryan Forbes, Dr Steve Chibnall of Demontford University, Richard Dacre of Flashbacks, and Dr Ian Smith for their help in supplying pictures. The photographs are credited where possible by film distributor and library source.

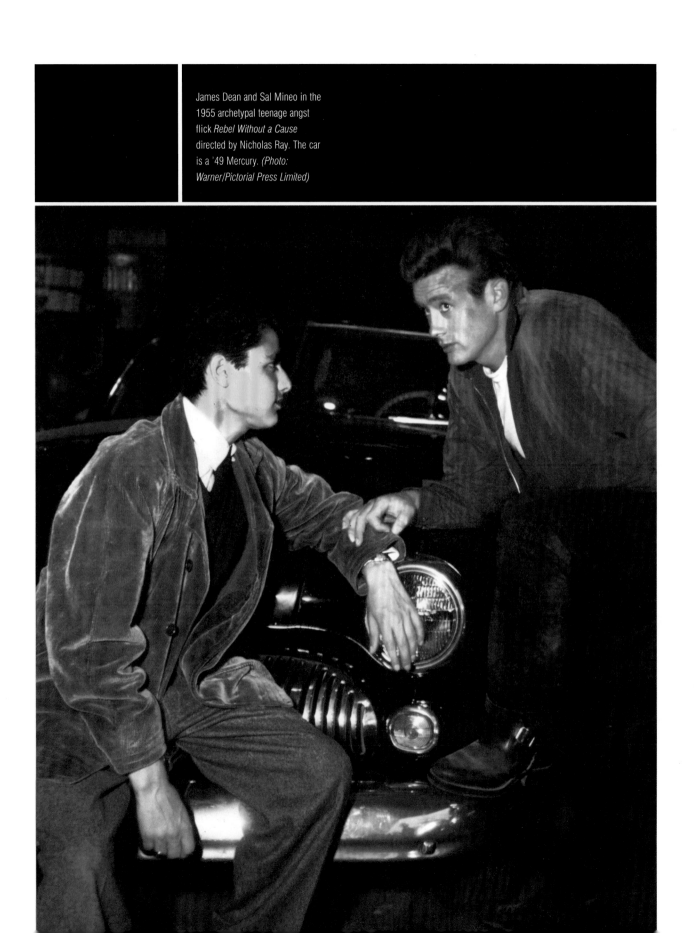

James Dean and Sal Mineo in the 1955 archetypal teenage angst flick *Rebel Without a Cause* directed by Nicholas Ray. The car is a '49 Mercury. *(Photo: Warner/Pictorial Press Limited)*

chapter one
on the road

journeys of significance

George C. Scott poses by
his BMW 503 Cabriolet in
The Last Run. (MGM/BFI)

A DEFINING CHARACTERISTIC of a 'road movie' is that the journey itself must be of crucial importance to the plot, be it long or short. This allows for films made outside the USA and Australia to be included, but it also means that films such as *Ice Cold in Alex*, which might otherwise have found a place in this section, have been put under 'The Car's The Star' because the importance of the vehicle itself largely outweighs the significance of the journey. Paradoxically, the true stars of films such as *Vanishing Point*, *Two-Lane Blacktop* and *Badlands* are the actual cars since it is the sole means by which their owners gain any sense of identity. Who would Warren Oates be, devoid of his Pontiac GTO? Do Martin Sheen and Sissy Spacek actually notice the Badlands of Montana as they drive cocooned with their pulp fantasies in a stolen Cadillac? Would *Goodbye Pork Pie* have been so watchable had the heroes used a Hillman Imp, or would the hollowness in Vittorio Gassman's life have been better demonstrated in *Il Sorpasso (The Easy Life)* had he driven an Alfa Romeo 2600 rather than a Lancia Aurelia, and would Jean-Paul Belmondo in *Pierrot le fou* have any sense of purpose were it not for wrecking imported Italian sports cars?

A sub-genre of road movies comprises those films in which the main protagonist goes native in their own country; a perpetual outsider seeking some form of truth. From the Rover P4-driving journalist exploring a service-station Britain in *Radio On* to the perpetually running Jack Nicholson in *Five Easy Pieces*, it is in the incidental detail that such films effortlessly convey a sense of angst (if that is not too strong a term). The short-haired locals in *Easy Rider*, reminding the viewer how distant the late 1960s now are (a time when long hair still meant a refusal to conform), the post-apocalyptic emptiness of Australia in *Mad Max*, or the utterly inept train heist attempt in *Bronco Billy* with Clint Eastwood's shoe salesman turned wild-west hero attempting to re-enact the efforts of Jesse James; albeit using a 20-year-old Pontiac Tempest convertible. One might even cite *Traffic* with Jacques Tati's persistent inventor in a converted Renault R4

battling with a chromium-plated landscape.

However, if the journey *per se* is the backbone of any road film, this does not imply that all such films must be about traversing continents; a British or a European road film is not a contradiction in terms. Such road films typically range from low-budget comedies like *Soft Top Hard Shoulder*, with a Herald 13/60 drophead, to art house films such as Wim Wenders's *Alice in den Städten (Alice in the Cities)*. As we have already suggested, the length of the actual journey can be largely immaterial.

Several New Wave British films contained sequences in which the protagonists journeyed to holiday resorts in order to escape the urban grime – Robert Stephens's Vauxhall Victor in *A Taste of Honey* is accompanied by an appropriately psuedo-American rock and roll soundtrack as it travels to Blackpool, whilst Richard Harris proudly takes his landlady and family on a trip in his newly acquired MkVII, oblivious to the fact that by 1963 his Jaguar is now heading towards banger status. From a distance of over four decades, what such 'kitchen sink' films now convey is a sense of stunted and limited ambition, combined with that other British staple – the dreadful holiday. *The Leather Boys* have no intention of taking over a small town à la Marlon Brando and friends in *The Wild One*; they just want to overtake Singer Gazelles in the rain. Similarly, in *The Loneliness of the Long Distance Runner* Tom Courtney and co. decide to take their 'birds' to the seaside in a Mk1 Consul. The presence of *The Likely Lads* film in this section is not through some warped sense of post-modern irony – the scenes of a caravan holiday with a Vauxhall Chevette are guaranteed to evoke terrible memories for those readers who lived in 1970s Britain.

Long before the heavily publicised *Kalifornia*, Ida Lupino directed *The Hitch-Hiker*, an unnerving confection of film noir and road movie in which two middle-class decent all-Americans on a fishing holiday are confronted by a mentally and physically scarred escaped convict. Lupino was virtually the only female director of an American film noir

15

Top, left: William Talman, Edmund O'Brien and Frank Lovejoy, with the solidly respectable 1950 Chrysler Windsor in *The Hitch-Hiker*. *(Photo: RKO Radio/Pictorial Press Limited)*

Top right: Psychotic foreman Patrick McGoohan (in left foreground) and fellow drivers lean on their lorries as new-boy Stanley Baker stands in *Hell Drivers*. *(Photo: Rank/Dr Steven Chibnall collection)*

Left: Gitane-smoking Jean-Paul Belmondo and Jean Seberg in Jean-Luc Godard's film *À bout de souffle* a.k.a. *Breathless*. Period Paris traffic of Simcas and Dauphines is a distraction. *(Photo: SNC/Pictorial Press Limited)*

and she expertly conveys the power games within the car as Frank Lovejoy and Edmond O'Brien – themselves both veterans of playing heavies – weigh up the odds of dispatching the unwelcome passenger. *The Hitch-Hiker* is one of a number of films where the journey and the passing landscape are secondary to the politics within the actual vehicle. *The Hitch-Hiker* has a separate entry, but there's also Tom Cruise and Dustin Hoffman in *Rain Man* (dare one suggest that Mr Cruise's performance was certainly equal to that of his co-star?); *Deadly Strangers* – after all it's not often that the term 'road movie' can be applied to a film that also contains Hayley Mills and the Austin Maxi; Spike Lee's *Get on the Bus*; Clint Eastwood and nephew in the 1930s-set *Honky Tonk Man* (although Kyle Eastwood's hair seems to belong to 1982); Ryan and Tatum O'Neal in *Paper Moon*; the gleeful degenerates in *Les Valseuses*; and the beguiling Finnish road movie/romantic comedy *Take Care of Your Handkerchief Tatiana* concerning two Russian ladies, two Finn rockabillies and a Volga Universal.

Alternatively, the journey in a film can be used to chart the changing relationship between the central protagonists. *Two for the Road* has a timescale that varies between the late 1950s and 1967 whilst *Last Orders* uses the trip to Dover in a Mercedes 500SEL to explore the nature of friendship and family ties. Meanwhile *Summer Holiday* – a film that has an equal claim to be considered together with any Peter Fonda epic – uses a journey across Europe to chart the changing nature of Sir Cliff Richard's taste in polyester shirts.

The Hitch-Hiker

US, 1953, 70mins, b&w
Dir: Ida Lupino

Mercifully, there's no Rutger Hauer in this treatment of the lasting bourgeois premise that they who have no car must be not merely poor but dangerous. The car here is a 1950 Chrysler and instead of taking a planned fishing trip the two occupants are forced at gunpoint by a killer to head for the Mexican border. One of the few film noirs directed by a woman.

Hell Drivers

GB, 1957, 108mins, b&w
Dir: C. Raker Endfield

Stanley Baker stars in this story of corruption and dangerous practice in a firm of hauliers. The main vehicular action takes the form of a fleet of Austin dumper trucks driven by a line-up of very familiar faces: Patrick McGoohan is Baker's main rival, both in the romance and lorry driving stakes. You'll also spot Sean Connery, Herbert Lom and David McCallum. The film bristles with Brylcreemed, square-jawed machismo in a pre-tachograph era.

À bout de souffle
(aka Breathless)

Fr, 1959, 87mins, b&w
Dir: Jean-Luc Godard

A sharply dressed young man, all fedora hat and Italian sports jacket, cruises a '58 Oldsmobile towards Paris. As the *voiture noveau riche* smoothly overtakes 203s and 2CV Camionettes, the camera constantly jump cuts between the Gitane-smoking driver and the tree-lined countryside. The young man then addresses the audience; 'If you don't like the sea and you don't like the mountains and you don't like the big city … then go hang yourself.'

Until this point in the film, the casual viewer might still be forgiven for taking *À bout de souffle* as another late 1950s French film noir B-movie. Michel, as played by Jean-Paul Belmondo, has to leave Marseilles in a hurry. Borrowing the Oldsmobile (and very unchivalrously abandoning his girlfriend in the process) he takes off for the capital where apparently he is owed money by the underworld. On the outskirts of Paris a gendarme flags him down but, having discovered a gun in the glove compartment, Michel guns down the policeman. No longer a petty thief, Michel is now a hunted desperado.

Alternatively, Michel is a young man so obsessed with the imagery of American gangster movies – the opening credits pay homage to Monogram films – that his own personality has been totally subsumed by fantasy. Certainly

After going off the road fleeing South American rebels, plantation boss David Niven saves Leslie Caron from the clutches of a bog which is claiming his '58 model Ford Ranch Wagon in *Guns of Darkness*. (Photo: ABP/Cavalcade)

Michel takes an equally childlike pleasure in both the gun and the Oldsmobile's electric windows but this one act of killing the police officer has caused the pseudo-Bogart mask to permanently fix.

However, even when thinking of a car in which to flee to Italy with his American 'moll' (Jean Seberg), Michel is still adolescent enough to consider several cars deemed appropriate for his persona – TR3, XK150 – before alighting on a white '57 Thunderbird for the doomed shoot-out.

Guns of Darkness

GB, 1962, 102mins, b&w
Dir: Anthony Asquith

The story of businessman/plantation boss, David Niven, and his wife Leslie Caron who, with rebels in pursuit, help an overthrown South American president in his bid to escape to the border. Features a '58 model Ford Ranch Wagon.

Summer Holiday

GB, 1962, 107mins, colour
Dir: Peter Yates

The plot of *Summer Holiday* is not terribly elaborate – Cliff and three other London Transport mechanics persuade their chums to convert a bus into a motor-caravan, working unpaid overtime for a week, so that Cliff and co. can enjoy a free holiday. This being 1962, and the spirit of Ealing not quite dormant, the gang is soon driving across Europe, continually stopping for pedestrian song-and-dance numbers. En route they encounter Una Stubbs and two other girlies in a 1932 Morris Minor Tourer. Naturally, being girlies they cannot drive and so Cliff and co. entice them onto the bus with a powerful display of erotic (for 1962) dancing. Later, they acquire another passenger – a 14-year-old 'boy' with a very visible bustline. It really was a more innocent age and it takes Cliff no little time to realise that

the 'boy' is a famous American chanteuse in disguise, being pursued by her mother in a rather nice white 1959 Thunderbird.

Several hundred song-and-dance numbers and changes of polyester shirt later, we finally arrive in Athens where the patient viewer can at last go Euro-Box spotting. Early '60s Athens traffic varies from 180D Pontons to late '40s Chevrolets, from Fiat 1900 Berlinas to even the odd Hillman Super-Minx, but alas we do not spend nearly long enough on this fascinating vista as the narrative must pack in a ballad and a rock-and-roll number before the happy ending. Cue closing credits and reprise of the theme song, leaving the viewer to speculate on the transformation of the singer of *Move It* and the attractively surly juvenile of *Expresso Bongo*. Yet, although *Summer Holiday* would appear a virtual museum piece by the time of *A Hard Day's Night*, its commercial and critical success did help to

preserve Cliff's image in amber – not as the Elvis clone of so many pre-Beatle British pop singers but as a recognisable figure in his own right.

Director Peter Yates moved on to bigger and better things with a definite car theme: *Robbery* and, of course, *Bullitt*.

The Leather Boys
GB, 1963, 108mins, b&w
Dir: Sidney J. Furie

More a bike than a car film, but we've given it room because we like it – so there. *The Leather Boys* captures the era of British bikes, ton-up boys and by-pass burn-ups like no other, though the central theme is of a working-class couple – Rita Tushingham and Colin Campbell – who marry too young, with a homoerotic sub-plot that gives a surprise twist at the end. The Ace Café on the old North Circular road looks fabulous, and Dudley Sutton is superb.

Bande à Part
(aka Band of Outsiders/The Outsiders)
Fr, 1964, 97mins, b&w
Dir: Jean-Luc Godard

Bande à Part, Godard's 1964 film featuring (in the director's own words) 'the suburban cousins of Michel' (see *À bout de souffle* on page 17) was shot in under a month and stars Godard's then wife and muse Anna Karina. *Bande* concerns itself with three fantasising young people (Karina, Claude Brasseur and Sami Frey) who decide to rob Mlle Karina's rich aunt.

Brasseur constantly dreams of driving Ferraris at Le Mans but, true to his suburban routes, drives a 1960 Facel Vega-bodied Simca Aronde convertible and practises not at a race track but at a builder's yard.

Pierrot le fou
(aka Crazy Pete/Pierrot Goes Wild)
Fr, 1965, 110mins, colour
Dir: Jean-Luc Godard

By 1965, Godard made what was possibly his last film with mainstream audience appeal, *Pierrot le fou*. Ferdinand Griffon (M. Belmondo) naturally tires of his bourgeois lifestyle – this is a Godard film – and leaves his wife and family to elope with his former babysitter (Mlle Karina). Unfortunately, there is a corpse in her apartment, and (anti) hero and heroine flee from gun-runners, thereby triggering a pretty decent car chase involving an Alfa Romeo 1600 Spyder and some musical numbers to boot.

Faster, Pussycat! Kill! Kill!
US, 1966, 83mins, b&w
Dir: Russ Meyer

Three massively endowed go-go girls head for the desert in their stick-shift euro sports cars – Porsche 356 cabriolet, MGA and TR3 – looking for kicks. Having declared war on mankind after years of being leered at in the club where they ply their trade, the plot unfolds into an orgy of mindless violence, bad dialogue and lingering cleavage shots.

Weekend
Fr, 1967, 105mins, colour
Dir: Jean-Luc Godard

In 1967's *Weekend* a decadent bourgeois couple, Corinne (Mirielle Darc) and Roland (Jean Yanne) set off to the countryside to visit Corrine's father in the hope of an inheritance – ideally Corinne's père might be involved in a car accident. Ironically, whilst en route, their Facel Vega Facilla is involved in an accident and the decadent duo are forced to walk through a rural France ravaged by hideous accidents involving Renualt R8s, Triumph TR4s, Citroën DS19s, Austin Minis and Panhard 24 Coupés. Not content with such scenes of automotive desecration, M. Godard also has Corinne et Roland harangued and humiliated by sundry revolutionaries – more than one film writer has noted that such a full-blooded assault on the couple actually tends to render them as not unsympathetic in addition to straying perilously close to nascent *Monty Python* territory. Anyway, on finally arriving at the family home, Roland and Corinne discover that Papa has died and left all to his widow. If that wasn't bad enough, Marxist revolutionaries then capture them. If the reader has received the impression that the writer is less than keen on this particular entry in the Godard canon he/she could be right. Maybe it's the destruction of all those cars.

Two for the Road
GB, 1967, 111mins, colour
Dir: Stanley Donen

Two for the Road features Audrey Hepburn in a Mercedes-Benz 250SL. For those few who require further recommendation of this film, it concerns a youngish married couple's journey through France, reflecting on the history of their marriage.

Initially we see Mr Finney as a young student with a blue MG TD, Audrey taking the minimal practicality in her stride – a youthful romantic adventure. The TD was also an appropriate choice since the pre-MGA models had not yet acquired their 'classic' status by the late 1950s. On their

The rare BMW 503 convertible with George C. Scott doing some explaining to the border police in *The Last Run*. (MGM/Author's collection)

Laurie Bird, James Taylor and Dennis Wilson pose with their 'breathed-on' 1955 Chevrolet from *Two-Lane Blacktop*. (Photo: Universal/BFI Collections)

honeymoon, the couple encounter a truly ghastly all-American suburban family straight from the warnings of Vance Packard, complete with Ford County Squire and obnoxious pig-tailed daughter. Finally, we arrive at the Mercedes-Benz stage in the relationship, for Finney is now a successful architect and although of honest blue-collar stock, far too innately tasteful to consider an E-type as the badge of his success. Audrey Hepburn belongs in a car with a white steering wheel.

The narrative avoids a linear progression – the viewer has to note the cars' tax discs and the changes in fashion to denote the actual period, as Frederick Raphael's narrative consists of vignettes moving between 1960 and 1967. Our heroes even encounter their own younger selves in the form of a red Triumph Herald 1200 Convertible, containing yet another young courting couple, but by the conclusion the relationship looks to be on stronger ground. After all, Mr Finney knows that he owns a Mercedes-Benz 250SL and is married to Audrey Hepburn. He truly is a lucky cad.

The Last Run
US, 1971, 92mins, colour
Dir: Richard Fleischer

This is the story of an ageing former Chicago gangster – George C. Scott – who retires to a Portuguese fishing village but agrees to come out of retirement to do one final job: smuggling an escaped convict across into Italy. Scott supplies the wheels: enter a blue BMW 503 convertible (one of only 412 made) which we see being lovingly fettled by George in the opening scenes of the film. The car features in almost every scene – which is just as well as it gives the film's most convincing performance, particularly during a hairy, dusty chase sequence where Scott and his co-stars are chased by rival hoods in a Series One Jaguar XJ6 in a very Continental shade of white. All the while our escaped baddy (played by Tony Musante) is hiding in a secret compartment behind the seats. To boost the V8's modest 160bhp, a supercharger is fitted and we hear it whine convincingly as the 503 pulls away from the Jag which may well have been one of the under-powered 2.8-litre tax break cars built specifically for Europe. Sadly, the supercharger was a mock-up – merely a dashboard switch and a fancy sound effect. It seems two 503s were used in the film – the one we see on screen and a camera car which was subsequently bought by a BMW enthusiast in West London and still sits in his garden, 30 years on, awaiting restoration. He was given it in payment for a job. The filming car is rolled by Scott at the end of a largely tiresome 93 minutes and the two old friends breathe their last together. Oops, spoiled it for you.

Two-Lane Blacktop
US, 1971, 103mins, colour
Dir: Monte Hellman

Two-Lane Blacktop was an attempt to make another Easy Rider but using four wheels as the means of transport rather than two. The singer/song-writer James Taylor was cast as the enigmatic hero, a man of few words but obviously an accomplished engineer who has built his own street racer based on a 1955 Chevrolet two-door. Those who know will notice the roll bar, the lack of chrome, the flared rear arches and the one piece flip-up front end with its massive hood scoop. Nobody says much about the engine but it seems to be a big block Chevy. Taylor and his sidekick prowl the highways and byways looking for other cars to race for pink slips. They encounter a big-mouthed driver of a Pontiac GTO (brilliantly played by Warren Oates) who agrees to race to Washington. Oates, with his factory-built muscle car, represents the straight world, and Taylor, with his hot rod and free-wheeling life style, the counter culture. James Taylor, despite an enigmatic performance (he's a man of few words) appears to have no further films to his credit. Look out for Beach Boy Dennis Wilson among the cast and a cameo by Harry Dean Stanton who later came to prominence in Repo Man. Director Monte Hellman seems to have done almost nothing worth mentioning since Two-Lane Blacktop although he is credited as the producer of Reservoir Dogs.

Vanishing Point

US, 1971, 107mins, colour

Dir: Richard C. Sarafian

A prerequisite of cult status seems to be that a film should flop on its initial release, then only really gain a following when exposed to a TV audience years later. So it was with *Vanishing Point*. 20th-Century Fox had very little faith in the film and only released it in local cinemas from whence it had disappeared within two weeks. It did much better in the UK where audiences warmed more readily to its existentialist themes. It was then re-released in the US in a double bill with *The French Connection* where it did much better business.

The storyline is misleadingly simple. Kowalski – former dirt-bike racer, stock car driver and cop – is now a delivery driver and has to drive a white 1970 Dodge Challenger from Denver to San Francisco in 15 hours, having just stepped out of a big Chrysler sedan at midnight. Popping amphetamines to keep himself awake, the exhausted Kowalski – played by Barry Newman who would be best remembered as Petrocelli the TV attorney with a social conscience who lived in a mobile home – is soon speeding in more ways than one, gunning the muscle car through the desert, occasionally making short off-road forays into

the sand to keep things interesting as he flashbacks through his life. At one point the Challenger passes the black Chrysler sedan on the road. It's Kowalski meeting himself coming back, and as the two cars pass the Challenger evaporates and we begin to understand that our hero is doomed.

Various things happen along the way: a race with a stripped-out E-type racer in the desert, giving a lift to two queens who are not as harmless as they appear and, in the original uncut 107-minute version, picking up Charlotte Rampling. She's dressed in black, shrouded in mist and holding a sign that says 'San Francisco'. They spend the night together in the desert and, before she mysteriously vanishes, Rampling warns the driver not to go to San Francisco. She was the symbol of death, but the patronising Fox bosses reckoned that US audiences wouldn't understand her significance, hence the cuts. With the state troopers on his tail Kowalski is now a marked man. His case is taken up by a blind local DJ who gives his listeners a running commentary on the pursuit. Somehow they develop an unspoken rapport through the radio, but when the two bulldozers appear in the road we are left in no doubt that Kowalski and the Challenger are going to meet a violent end against their shovels.

Left: Barry Newman in the Dodge Challenger dicing with the stripped-down E-type in *Vanishing Point*.
(Photo: TCF/Cupid/Pictorial Press Limited)

Right: A stunt driver throwing a Ford Galaxie from *The Getaway* at someone's front porch with destructive results.
(Photo: Solar/First Artists/Pictorial Press Limited)

Deliverance
US, 1972, 109mins, colour
Dir: John Boorman

Burt Reynolds offers a superior version of Hollywood's alienated-white-hero-plus-macho-vehicle device in a film that brought new meaning to the phrase 'male bonding'. The car is a Ford Bronco off-roader – a much earlier and more spartan model than the one famously used by O. J. Simpson in his televised gun-to-temple flight from the LAPD.

The Getaway
US, 1972, 122mins, colour
Dir: Sam Peckinpah

An opportunity for director Sam Peckinpah and hell-raiser Steve McQueen to indulge their respective penchants for slow-motion violence and fast-motion driving, leaving Roger Donaldson's 1994 reprise with Alec Baldwin and Kim Basinger trailing in their wake.

Badlands
US, 1973, 95mins, colour
Dir: Terrence Malick

Badlands, loosely based around the Starkweather-Fugate murders of 1958, is the story of a teenage girl (Holly) and young garbage collector (Kit) who wander across America in a 1959 Cadillac Eldorado leaving a trail of death and mayhem. It is one of the finest American films made in the 1970s. Why? Well, just consider the following sequence. Kit (Martin Sheen) and Holly (Sissy Spacek) have holed up at the shack of one Cato, a friend and co-worker of Kit. However, Kit being a suspicious sort shoots Cato in the stomach and as he dies in agony the young couple amiably converse with him.

Holly's voiceover blandly and emotionlessly justifies Kit's actions. Then, unexpectedly, another couple arrive in a Studebaker Commander (for a low budget movie, the period cars are really well chosen). Kit eventually dispatches them too as Holly passively observes.

On leaving the house (wearing the owner's white fedora) Kit now has the choice of two getaway vehicles; the red Roll-Royce Silver Cloud and the black Cadillac Eldorado, and naturally he chooses the Cadillac. As we have already seen, Kit's self-image is a less-than-beguiling combination of rebel without a cause together with Eisenhower-era upright and buttoned-down patriotism ('he was very fastidious … people who littered bothered him.') Even the colour of the stolen Eldorado is perfect for Kit – not a candy pink Cadillac celebrated in Elvis Presley and Carl Perkins records but a solidly respectable black. Aside from that, the American car's suspension will be better suited to the Badlands of South Dakota as the couple start their drift towards the Montana border.

As Holly's vapid narration fills in the empty time by reading insipid drivel from Hollywood fanzines, Kit pilots the Cadillac across the treeless plains whilst constantly striking James Dean-like poses. For food Kit 'occasionally rams a cow', for fuel he raids a gas pipeline. As they sight the Saskatchewan mountains along the Canadian border, Malick cuts to a shot of the Eldorado's four headlamps cutting through the desert night as the car spreads out clouds of dust. Inside the Cadillac, the instrument lights illuminate Kit's blank features as he fantasises about joining the RCMP. A dove crosses the path of the headlights and Kit and Holly dance in front of their stolen car to the tune of Nat King Cole's *A Blossom Fell*.

The end, both of the pursuit and relationship, is nigh. The next day, in the midst of the High Plains of Montana, Holly leaves and surrenders to a police helicopter whilst Kit fires on one of the state troopers and roars off. Whilst re-fuelling at a Texaco station, a passing Sheriff's car recognises Kit from TV and newspaper reports, and gives chase.

Kit's response to the pursuing squad car is wholly typical; whilst expertly driving the Cadillac off the highway and onto dirt roads, crashing through cow fences and producing clouds of dust, he still finds the time to adjust his door mirror to check his own reflection. But without his near-mute witness, what is the point of such bravado – even if the police car is temporarily stalled after rolling on its side – so Kit halts the Cadillac and shoots out a tyre. Donning the Cadillac owner's white hat, Kit waits calmly on the front bonnet for the arrival of the Sheriff.

Dirty Mary Crazy Larry
US, 1974, 92mins, colour
Dir: John Hough
At 34 Peter Fonda was still young enough to cut the mustard as a virile anti-establishment hero in *Easy Rider*

mould. Hero is probably the wrong word as none of the three main characters in *Dirty Mary Crazy Larry* are especially likeable. Here Fonda (Larry) swaps a Hog for the inevitable Dodge Charger and plays a small-time local racing driver who has the talent for bigger things but not the money. So he robs a supermarket, picks up airhead groupie Susan George (still trendy enough not to have to slum-it in *EastEnders*) and embarks on a nihilistic 100-mile chase across the Californian landscape, out-driving the local cops. The film contains 18 separate car crashes, a head-on collision with a train, a draw bridge jump, a crash through an advertisement hoarding, endless roll-overs and even a crash into a helicopter.

Engaging for most of its 92 minutes and makes it easily into any top ten of car chase films.

Les Valseuses
Fr, 1974, 150mins, colour
Dir: Bernard Blier
Gerard Depardieu and Patrick Dewaere as two young degenerates who take our young heroine on a road trip through France, pausing only for bouts of troilism and sodomy, between borrowing quite a variety of French cars – from the now nearly forgotten Renault 12 (as used by the Romanian Ambassador to the UK no less) to a post-war Citroën Traction. This last named is swapped for a very late model DS Pallas, property of a bank manager and his family. Gerard and Patrick, being the chivalrous chaps that they are, leave the family their Traction Avant and then deflower their (willing) teenaged daughter whilst Miou-Miou regards the pair benevolently. Unsurprisingly, *Les Valseuses* was a huge French box office success. Just ask any French-speaking friend to translate the title for you.

Race with the Devil
US, 1975, 88mins, colour
Dir: Jack Starrett
Diabolists give Peter Fonda and Loretta (TV Hotlips) Switt the Winnebago caravan trip from Hell – literally.

The Gumball Rally

US, 1976, 102mins, colour
Dir: Chuck Bail

The Gumball Rally was marginally the most watchable of a whole spate of indulgent, star-studded *Wacky Races* style road movies that emerged out of Hollywood in the 1970s but it's still only worth enduring for the cars. These include a Mercedes 300SL roadster, AC Cobra, E-type, Silver Shadow and Ferrari Daytona Spider which are involved in a 2,900 mile, 34-hour race across the States.

The Likely Lads

GB, 1976, 90mins, colour
Dir: Michael Tuchner

As 1970s British sit-com spin-offs go, this is one of the best of a very very dismal bunch, despite the screenplay's lapse into Brian Rix territory towards the final reel. The sight of up-and-coming Bob and 1960s throwback Terry in the former's new Chevette L (complete with plaid cloth upholstery and reclining front seats – a worthy replacement for the series's HB Viva De-Luxe) taking their partners to Hadrian's Wall for a truly dismal winter break is enough to evoke depressing memories in anyone old enough to remember 1976. The meticulous Bob collects Green Shield stamps at Shell stations and is forever losing his wing mirrors when parking at Terry's council estate. The trip to the deserted seaside resort encapsulates the film; 1970s British sit-com meets 1950s kitchen sink drama. Incidentally, Alun Armstrong who plays the milkman should be familiar to *Get Carter* fans – he played Keith the barman.

Smokey and the Bandit

US, 1977, 91mins, colour
Dir: Hal Needham

American cinema seemed to have an obsession in the '70s with hick anti-establishment figures driving either trucks (*Convoy* with Kris Kristofferson) or muscle cars (anything with Burt Reynolds). This was the first of an all too long series of *Smokey* films and really the only watchable one: the stunts are its saving grace, while Sheriff Buford T. Justice is quite fun to watch.

The Cannonball Run
Cannonball Run II

US, 1980/83, 95/108mins, colour
Dir: Hal Needham

This indulgent '70s-hangover dross is a kind of real-life *Wacky Races*, featuring an assortment of stars who appear to be enjoying a private joke. Burt Reynolds is involved along with Roger Moore, Henry Fonda, Dean Martin, the then fashionable Farah Fawcett and Sammy Davis Jr who presumably would attend the opening of an envelope by this stage in his career. The premise of the whole affair was a real-life annual coast-to-coast race conceived by the famous *Car and Driver* writer Brock Yates. Look out for Daytona Spiders and Mercedes 300SL Gullwings among the four-wheeled stars. Director Hal Needham was a former stuntman, which explained a lot. He'd already done the first two *Smokey and the Bandit* films. See also *The Gumball Rally* (1976) which is very much of the same ilk.

Top: Sheriff Buford T. Justice (Jackie Gleason) in one of the many crash scenes from *Smokey and the Bandit*. The cars are Oldsmobiles.
(Photo: Universal/Rastar/Pictorial Press Limited)

Bottom: A publicity poster for *The Cannonball Run*. Although Mr Chan had a low billing, he got to drive a Subaru Justy, lucky chap.
Right: A stunt man done up to look like Roger Moore, being fired from the ejector seat of one of the ex-*Goldfinger* DB5s in *The Cannonball Run*.
(Photos: Golden Harvest/Pictorial Press Limited)

You'll root for them all... but you'll never guess who wins.

THE CANNONBALL RUN

GOLDEN HARVEST PRESENTS AN ALBERT S. RUDDY PRODUCTION A HAL NEEDHAM FILM

BURT REYNOLDS
ROGER MOORE
FARRAH FAWCETT
"THE CANNONBALL RUN"
DOM DeLUISE · DEAN MARTIN
SAMMY DAVIS, Jr.
JACKIE CHAN · MICHAEL HUI
ADRIENNE BARBEAU · JAMIE FARR

Executive Producer RAYMOND CHOW Produced by ALBERT S. RUDDY Written by BROCK YATES
Directed by HAL NEEDHAM Music Conducted by AL CAPPS
Music Supervision by SNUFF GARRETT

Goodbye Pork Pie

NZ, 1981, 105mins, colour
Dir: Geoff Murphy

Gerry, a teenaged punk rocker and all-round beatnik, hires a yellow Mini 1000 – using a stolen credit card and fake driving licence – to travel the length of New Zealand. En route, he acquires the middle-aged John who is desperately trying to visit his estranged partner. Soon enough, Gerry's interesting driving technique earns the pair a lot of police attention and the sobriquet 'The Blondini Gang'.

This is one of the most intelligent uses of a Mini since *The Italian Job* and proof that the vast open spaces of Australia or the USA are not essential for a good road film. Aside from that, Hollywood films such as *Convoy* or *Smokey and the Bandit* don't feature nearly as many Singer Vogues and HD Holdens as does this New Zealand production.

Pink Cadillac

US, 1989, 122mins, colour
Dir: Buddy Van Horn

Clint's a bounty hunter; Bernadette Peters is a mother who has disappeared with $250,000 in a pink 1959 Cadillac Eldorado which some nasty neo-Nazi people would like to get back.

Rain Man

US, 1990, 133mins, colour
Dir: Barry Levinson

Dustin Hoffman and Tom Cruise drive their father's Buick Roadmaster convertible to Las Vegas in this story of a yuppie Lamborghini and Ferrari dealer who is united with an autistic brother he didn't know he had. The actual Buick used, with its straight-eight engine and Dynaflow transmission, later found its way to a car dealer in Manchester.

Thelma and Louise

US, 1991, 129mins, colour
Dir: Ridley Scott

Brad Pitt contemplates Geena Davis and Susan Sarandon's 1964 Ford Thunderbird, which has already witnessed one car-park shooting of a trucker (truckers don't come out of this film very well) who took the girls lightly. After shooting the potential rapist the women go on the run from the cops (led by Harvey Keitel) on an adventure in the desert with the T-Bird running away not only from the alleged offence but from their boring jobs and the men in their lives. The girls give Pitt a lift, and he takes Geena Davis for a ride in every possible sense before leaving them penniless. In Britain a series of Peugeot ads set out to capitalise on the film's near-definitive images of post-feminist sisterhood but somehow a 307 Diesel doesn't have quite the romance of a Thunderbird. Despite the drama of the well-known airborne ending and its commentary, and the nature of some men (well truckers really), *Thelma and Louise* is upbeat and optimistic.

Kalifornia

US, 1993, 118mins, colour
Dir: Dominic Sena

Despite the lovely Juliette Lewis, a clap-door Lincoln Continental is perhaps the most authentic thing in this attempt to recreate *Badlands* for the '90s. Critics liked the look of the film but found the violence flowed too easily and the feel was pretentious, but it's probably worth watching for the clap-door Lincoln, one of the most well used icons of 1960s American design in cinema. Its numerous appearances would almost warrant a book to themselves.

british comedy

crooks, crocs and new elizabethans

THERE IS A MINOR SCENE in *Genevieve* – it's the first occasion on the journey to Brighton that the Darracq breaks down, and whilst John Gregson investigates and Dinah Sheridan looks out the coffee flask a modern saloon pulls up alongside and its driver leans across and makes a witty remark. The car is a grey A40 Somerset and the point here is that had it survived (maybe it did) the Austin would now be the same age as the veteran Darracq was in 1953 when the film was released. That puts *Genevieve* in period piece territory – an example of British cinema heritage. It also means that the contemporary background cars are now of just as much, or more, interest than the actual veterans the story is built around.

Incidentally, this scene was shot at a place called Batchworth Heath beyond the north-west suburbs of London, and the entrance arch to Moor Park Golf Club can be seen in the background – not exactly on a direct route between London and Brighton.

Genevieve is what some film writers call a 'New Elizabethan' comedy. The 'New Elizabethan' respects heritage (veteran cars, steam engines, James Robertson-Justice in any form) and looks forward to a jolly future – often in a London where young people could actually afford to live and in superbly photographed colour too.

Doctor in the House, made in the following year, has all of these attributes – particularly the very choice Bentleys and Lagondas – and was frequently double-billed with *Genevieve* – 'The Doc & The Croc!'

It has an added bonus for ambulance enthusiasts – a chase sequence involving a Barker-bodied Daimler in which rather elderly undergraduates, piled on the running boards of various jalopies, are pursued by yet more undergraduates (aged 30-something) in the Daimler. Sadly we do not have the space to consider what would happen if, for argument's sake, a gang of welders from Lambeth tried the same stunt.

To more readily analyse the types of cars that appear in British comedies of the fifties and sixties it might be useful to explore the different characters that drove them.

The post-war wide boy was last seen in all his glory in 1954's *The Belles of St Trinians*, but the comic villain persisted and he would be played by Sydney Tafler, Harry Fowler, Michael Medwin or George Cole. He had to drive an American or pseudo-American car – A105s, Crestas or Zodiacs would suffice if a Chevrolet was not available.

James Robertson-Justice, of course, in a succession of venerable Rolls-Royces. The Silver Wraith in *Doctor in Love* is particularly enviable.

As with *Doctor in the House* or *Bachelor of Hearts*, the student or newly qualified chap, to display his carefree spirit, drives a vehicle that is at least 20 years old. Alternatively, as with Nicholas Parsons in *Brothers-in-Law*, he might build his own Lotus 7.

However, with maturity comes wisdom, cardigans, pipe-smoking and very dull cars. Michael Craig, whom Rank attempted to promote as a second string Bogarde, used a battleship grey Zephyr-six Mk2 in *Upstairs & Downstairs* – but never a Zodiac. In *Dentist on the Job*, a film from Bob Monkhouse's brief career as a cinema comedian, he drives a Minor 1000 Convertible. *Weekend with Lulu* (see 'The Car's the Star') saw Bob in France with a Bedford Dormobile.

But what of Dr Simon Sparrow himself? For his final 'Doctor' film, Dirk Bogarde boasts a Morris Mini-Minor Super with wickerwork panels. However, if this is an attempt to make Dirk look hip in *Doctor in Distress* it fails largely because Bogarde is so bored, waspish and frankly over-age in the part. Still, any film that features Samantha Eggar with a Maserati 3500GT can't be devoid of merit.

The cad may be a cheat, a womaniser and a welsher but he is always immaculately dressed, has the best dialogue and drives the choicest cars. In *Happy Ever After* of 1954 David Niven plays the squire and soon proves his caddish credentials: not only does he evict tenants he also swaps his Rolls-Royce 20/25 Shooting Brake for an Allard. But the cad's cad has to be Terry-Thomas.

In *The Green Man*, a tale of international assassins and mad BBC announcers in suburbia, Alistair Sim uses a Minx Californian as part of his cover, whilst commercial traveller George Cole drives a Mk1 Zephyr, but these worthy vehicles are soon forgotten when T-T arrives in an XK140 at said hotel for a dirty weekend with Dora Bryan. T-T in an XK140 was such a good combination that it was repeated in *Too Many Crooks* the following year.

For the finest example of Decent Chap v Cad look no further than *School for Scoundrels*. Decent chap Ian Carmichael (the chap's chap) rivals T-T (who else) for the heart of Janette Scott. But T-T drives a 'Bellini' – actually a disguised Lagonda – whilst Carmichael is conned by two car dealers, Morris and Dudley Grosvenor (Dennis Price and Peter Jones), into buying a semi-derelict Bentley 3-litre. It is only after a course at Alistair Sim's School of Lifemanship that Carmichael turns the tables on the 'Winsome Welshmen' and trades in the Bentley for an Austin Healey 3000 Mk1. In the light of current values it would have been wiser to have kept the Bentley, but in 1960 who would have realised that?

The following scene from *Please Turn Over* exemplifies the attitude of British film comedy towards the lady motorist. Lionel Jeffries is teaching Jean Kent to drive in his 100E Anglia. Naturally she simpers a great deal and is utterly useless at the wheel – 'Lor lummee, she's coming back!', cries a chirpy cockney navvy as Ms Kent careers down a country lane. Not being content with this 'hilarious' moment, Gerald Thomas (director) also gave us 1963's *Nurse on Wheels* which starts with Nurse Juliet Mills attempting to pass her driving test in an A40 Farina. Although this is a slight improvement on the Anglia – at least the Austin has electric wipers – and the film does give younger viewers a glimpse of the pre-1976 days when hand signals were part of the driving test, the screenplay still requires Miss Mills to simper and twitter.

Still, *Nurse on Wheels* is interesting for giving the heroine a white Mini-Minor Super as her official car – British

films of the early sixties often had young professionals in Minis; Derek Nimo's GP in *The Bargee* being another good example – and it also has Jim Dale giving a demonstration of how to use a starting handle on a Phase 1 Vanguard. But for those who yearn for a film which treats female motorists with a modicum of respect, there is virtually only one choice – *The Fast Lady*: we will deal with this in detail later.

British comedy was running out of steam by the late sixties. The comic mainstays – *St Trinians*, Norman Wisdom, *Doctor*, and the *Carry Ons* – either faded away after 1966 or, as with the *Carry Ons*, were starting to live on borrowed time. Whilst 1969's *Carry on Camping* does have its moments – wonderfully unconvincing hippies with their Mini-Moke (British cinema ALWAYS had flower children in Mini-Mokes) plus Windsor's bra – as soon as Sid James acquired his Marina 1.8 Super in *At Your Convenience*, the series was doomed.

All sense of nostalgia is completely dissipated as soon as the Marina, that harbinger of 1970s ghastliness, hoves into view (apparently Sid was actually given the car and promptly sold it for gambling funds – a fitting response). The Marina OC may argue that it is a much maligned car, but for me the Marina marked the gateway to that dreaded celluloid abyss that is the 'Confessions' film series of 1973–1977, the 'Adventures' series and the other sundry dregs of British cinema.

As far as cars are concerned, there are few of note – the films' *raison d'être* was full-frontal female nudity to lure the mackintoshed cinema goer but *Confessions of a Driving Instructor* does boast a Mk2 Cortina Super with a floor gear change and Webasto roof … useful for getting an overhead shot of the front seat action with homely TV Oxo cube mum Linda Bellingham.

Tony Booth starred alongside Robin Askwith in the majority of these soft porn comedies. Booth was best known as the 'Scouse Git' from the Alf Garnett TV series but never found his feet in films.

However, apart from the sight of Tony Blair's father-in-law displaying his bare backside, the 'Confessions' have all the appeal of a 1974 Hillman Hunter De-Luxe with PVC trim.

Kay Kendall, up to her calves in a ford, having to push the Spyker while Kenneth More shouts instructions from the driving seat in *Genevieve*. Such were the joys of early motoring. *(Photo: Rank)*

Genevieve

GB, 1953, 86mins, colour
Dir: Henry Cornelius

Genevieve is one of the most important films in this book. Without *Genevieve*, the British classic car movement may have taken an entirely different form.

Rank wanted the film to star Dirk Bogarde and Claire Bloom. The fourth-billed Kenneth More wrote that he was paid a flat fee of £2,500 for his five-month stint. *Genevieve* started shooting in October 1952 – the London–Brighton Rally sequences are genuine – and was completed by February 1953.

Alan McKim (John Gregson) is a young barrister who lives in a mews cottage, for *Genevieve* was made in the days when embryonic professionals could actually aspire to live in the capital. His pride and joy is his Darracq (Genevieve) and as he sets off in her along the Strand Cornelius's cunning becomes apparent. The hero of any 1950s comedy must defer to both authority and tradition and by framing our heroine in such surroundings, the film implies that a veteran car is definitely an integral part of Britain's heritage. His wife Wendy (Diana Sheridan) is semi-convinced that Alan prefers the Darracq's charms to her own, and to raise the sexual temperature a little higher we also meet the Spyker-driving Ambrose Claverhouse (Kenneth More in the role that moulded his film career), an advertising agent.

Once we reach the start of the London–Brighton, veteran car enthusiasts should reach for the pause button whilst readers of a certain age will recognise Mr Movietone Newsreels himself, Leslie Mitchell, from the days when media commentators rode the countryside in Ford V8 station wagons. We also meet Ambrose's new girlfriend Rosalind (Kay Kendall). In amongst the flotillas of black pre-war Austin 10s and Vauxhall 14s, we can see the odd Minor, Zephyr-Six and the Kafkaesque Phase 1 Vanguard. District Nurses drive pre-war Morris 8 Tourers and henpecked little men (Reginald Beckwith) borrow their wife's vermilion Allard K1.

On the return journey the two parties decide to stage a private race, allowing the viewer to witness an England straight from the pages of a Ladybird book. Policemen still directed the traffic on point duty, middle-aged women can't drive their 1938 Minx Tourers and costermongers' barrows are there to be overturned. Ice cream men still ride tricycles and sell 'strawberry cream ices' for 3d, whilst public telephones can only be operated by pressing Button A. As in all the best British films, character actors inhabit even the smallest cameo, from Michael Medwin to Edie Martin, from Geoffrey Keen to Joyce Grenfell. It has Kay Kendall miming to Kenny Baker's trumpet, a degree of sexual sophistication rare in post-war British comedy. It is the keystone to many a classic car magazine and, above all, is celluloid proof that nostalgia is not necessarily a negative emotion. All this from a Darracq found in a junkyard in 1945.

Two Way Stretch

GB, 1960, 87mins, b&w

Dir: Robert Day

Two Way Stretch, being set in a gaol, obviously features fewer vehicles than *The Wrong Arm*. There are prison-vans, of course – Morris-Commercials, the GPO still run Morris 8s and the army still use Austin Champs. The prison mini-bus is a Morris J2, whose squat shape used to fill suburban high streets. The plot – three prisoners break out of gaol, steal some gems and break back in for the perfect alibi – is subordinate to the acting. Sellers is smooth and cagey as the gang leader, Wilfred Hyde-White as his outside contact appears as a bogus clergyman, complete with Morris Minor Convertible and hail-fellow-well-met mannerisms and Liz Fraser drives an Aston Martin DB MkIII drophead.

The Fast Lady

GB, 1962, 95mins, colour

Director: Ken Annakin

Ken Annakin is remembered for *Those Magnificent Men in Their Flying Machines* but between 1960 and 1964 he made four fine comedies starring Leslie Phillips, Stanley Baxter and James Robertson-Justice, of which *The Fast Lady* was the first in colour. The star of the title? – a Bentley 3-litre.

From the opening credits, the true motoring enthusiast knows that this is going to be top entertainment – a trad jazz theme tune plus a list of guest stars from John Surtees and Graham Hill to Frankie Howerd and Raymond Baxter. The story starts with Stanley Baxter being knocked off his bicycle by a Bentley S2 Continental drophead driven by curmudgeonly car magnate JRJ. On going to JRJ's house Stanley is given a lift home by JRJ's daughter, Julie Christie, in her red and black Morris-Cooper. Ms Christie is an expert driver (a real rarity for an early 1960s British film) and this inspires Stanley to consider buying a car. As fortune would have it he shares rooms with spivvy car dealer Leslie Phillips. We see Phillips at work, trying to off-load Healey 100/4s and TR2s onto a terrified punter, and only clinging to his job by palming off 'The Old Sputnik' – i.e. the Bentley –

to his room-mate: £500 changes hands and Stanley now owns the 3-litre. Unfortunately he cannot drive.

So, Stanley visits your average school of motoring run by neurotic Eric Barker. The lesson not being adjudged a success, Phillips himself teaches Stanley to drive in the Bentley for both have an interest in passing the test – Stanley has fallen in love with Ms Christie and Leslie wants the contract to sell JRJ's cars. Neither will come to pass if JRJ has any say in the matter unless Stanley can drive the Fast Lady to JRJ's standards. Our hero dreams of driving the Bentley at Goodwood and, courtesy of the wonders of Pinewood back projection, we see Stanley race the Bentley against Hill and Surtees whilst Raymond Baxter and John Bolster commentate.

Naturally the day of the test doesn't go well, but as Stanley approaches the test centre we see a white MkVIIM Jaguar pull up outside the bank. Michael Balfour and Danny Green get out, both clad in dark suits and trilbies. The Jaguar may as well have had 'Villains' written across the front. A PC, oblivious to the 'L' plates, commandeers the Fast Lady and orders Stanley to follow the Jaguar, his colleague doing likewise with Leslie, Julie and JRJ in the James Young Continental Drophead S2. The chase is on, subsequently joined by 716 TPD, a police 6/99 that made more appearances than many character actors.

Stanley initially gives whirly turning-left signals but after being told 'to hell with the highway code' by the plod on the rear seat, starts to drive like a complete cad. The villains take a short cut through a golf course and the chase intensifies as the four cars enter the Motorway construction site. Annakin, by mixing more back-projection shots of the grimly determined Stanley with footage of stunt driving, ends the chase with Baxter forcing the Jaguar off the road. Stanley is allowed the hand of Julie in marriage by JRJ and everyone lived happily ever after.

Leslie Phillips was offered the Fast Lady for £350 after filming and turned it down. A Bentley 3-litre for less than half the price of a new Hillman Super-Minx; don't you ever have the impression that you were born too late?

Below: Graham Hill being chased by a back-projected Bentley in Stanley Baxter's dream sequence from *The Fast Lady*.
Bottom left: That Bentley again, this time with 'L' plates and getting dangerously near the man painting a line on the road.
(Photo: Rank/Group Films)

Bottom right shows Julie Christie learning to drive The Fast Lady. Her terrified passenger isn't Leslie Phillips but unsung stunt hero Jack Silk (see cops & robbers).
(Photo: Rank/Group Films)

Michael Craig (with manly pipe) giving Anne Helm a ticking-off for driving her Cadillac too fast along narrow English lanes in *The Iron Maiden*. (Photo: Rank/Pictorial Press Limited)

Peter Sellers and Mai Zetterling in a clinch on the reclined seats of an Oldsmobile convertible in *Only Two Can Play*. (Photo: British Lion/Vale/Pictorial Press Limited)

Right: Arthur Mullard (as Brass Knuckles in *The Wrong Arm of the Law*) shouting from the passenger window of Peter Sellers's Aston Martin DB4 GT Vantage. (Photo: Romulus/Robert Verlaise/BFI Films)

The Iron Maiden

GB, 1962, 98mins, colour

Dir: Gerald Thomas

The maiden is a traction engine owned by Alvis TD-driving aircraft designer Michael Craig. We watch a US airline's attempt to buy a British plane being thwarted by Craig and the airline boss's daughter who drives a Cadillac.

Only Two Can Play

GB, 1962, 106mins, b&w

Dir: Sydney Gilliat

Based on Kingsley Amis's *That Uncertain Feeling*, this film – made in an era when electric windows were rare – allowed Sellers and Mae Zetterling to explore, in Wales, the uses of an Oldsmobile convertible. It tells the story of a very married librarian who falls in love with a councillor's wife. The Oldsmobile could well have been Sellers' own car as he was in the habit of changing them every week at this stage.

On the Beat

GB, 1962, 101mins, b&w

Dir: Robert Asher

Norman Wisdom is convinced that he should join the London Met, despite his height of 5ft 2ins. After the trad-jazz opening theme we cut to a 6/90 Traffic Car, equipped with one of the new blue beacons, speeding through goods yards. It pulls up alongside 716TPD, to reveal Superintendent Pitkin. Naturally, it is a dream since Pitkin's job at the Yard is to clean the Flying Squad's Hawks and 6/99s – inevitability, he loses this job by drenching the Commissioner Raymond Huntley and causing John Blythe to crash a Silver Cloud SII into the boss's Silver Wraith in a really very painful scene for car lovers.

The Wrong Arm of the Law

GB, 1962,94mins, b&w

Dir: Cliff Owen

This is a near-perfect comedy about Australian police impersonators and the aggravation they cause to both the underworld and the genuine police in London. It was written by Galton and Simpson of *Steptoe and Son* fame. Peter Sellers, in a superb double-role, plays West End couturier Monsieur Jules, a front for gang-boss 'Pearly' Gates. Naturally Gates wants to put an end to the Australian firm's activities, and after liaising with rival crime lynchpin 'Nervous O'Toole' (Bernard Cribbins with a James Young-bodied S2 fitted with then unheard of rear seat belts just to underline his nerves) he approaches Scotland Yard to arrange a temporary truce so that they can join forces to solve the problem. If you look closely you'll spot Michael Caine as a young copper.

This chaotic collaboration spurs the narrative into an excellent chase sequence for the final two reels, chiefly memorable for a genuine Met car, a Series III 6/90, attempting to keep pace with Gates's DB4 Vantage (Sellers's own car in real life), the police driver gamely wrestling with the steering wheel and clanging the gong. In fact, the whole film is a nice evocation of a post-*Lavender Hill Mob* London, with Nanette Newman in a Sprite MkII, Commer Karrier ice cream vans, haberdashers in Morris J2s and, of course, Joe Wadham in 716 TPD. This last is Inspector 'Nosey' Parker's (Lionel Jeffries) own squad car, which the Australians hijack, and later abandon in the Commissioner's parking space.

A Stitch in Time

GB, 1963, 89mins, b&w

Dir: Robert Asher

A Stitch in Time veers far more towards pathos – Pitkin comforting an orphaned girl – but Wisdom is a good enough actor to make the scenes work. It also has his two most famous straight men – Edward 'Mr. Grimsdale' Chapman and Jerry Desmonde. But for car enthusiasts, there is a brace of choice moments. The first is when Norman, bandaged for a St. John demonstration (don't ask), contrives to ride on the roof of a 1953 Austin ambulance. The second involves a Hillman Imp De-Luxe press car. He manages to crash the car whilst dressed as a female nurse (again, don't ask). Pitkin makes a final speech that brings tears to the eyes of everyone who isn't a banger-racer or an estate agent.

Carry On Cabby

GB, 1963, 90mins, b&w

Dir: Gerald Thomas

For Britons of a certain age, the *Carry On* films are more a part of their televisual heritage than an early experience of cinema-going. In the1980s, examples of the genre – up to 1964's *Spying* – would serve as a Sunday BBC1 matinee, or alternate with the *Matt Helm* epics on the BBC2 evening schedule. The average *Carry On* did not provide much of interest for the juvenile car-spotter – the low budget precluded retakes so it could hardly be expected to extend to car chases. The pursuit in *Constable*, between a 1950 De Soto getaway car and a commandeered A30 wages van (!), lasts for less than two minutes. In terms of transport Sid drives a 1961 Consul 375 in *Camping*; a 1964 Zodiac Mk.III in *Matron*; and a Marina 1.8 Super in *At Your Convenience*. Allegedly, Sid was given the Morris in real life and promptly exchanged it for gambling funds – the only real option.

Carry On Cabby was the first in the series to be penned by Talbot Rothwell. Originally he was contracted to write *Call Me A Cab*, as the film was not envisaged as a *Carry On* proper but, after a none-too-successful release, executive producer Peter Rogers quickly re-branded the film.

The opening credits are played over Sid ferrying Ian Wilson in his 1957 Austin FX3 to the strains of Eric Roger's very jolly theme music. We subsequently learn that Sid owns Speedee Cabs, which comprises a fleet of FX3s – not an FX4 to be seen. He is a genial workaholic who neglects his wife Peggy (Hattie Jacques). Peggy, together with Liz Fraser, decides to use her savings to set up a rival taxi firm, in order to save her marriage (no one could ever accuse a *Carry On* film of suffering from a plausible or under-elaborate plot) and it is here that the credit giving thanks to the Ford Motor Company makes perfect sense. Even if you haven't seen the film – unlikely as that may seem – you must have caught one particular sequence on TV programmes dealing with 1960s affluence, sexual emancipation or mass transport in the UK.

The cars that Peggy uses for her new firm are Consul-Cortina Supers – courtesy of the Ford GB Press Fleet – and

the name of the firm is Glamcabs. As Hattie, Liz and Esma Cannon walk down the ranks of Valerie Van Ost, Amanda Barrie and their fellow Glamcabs drivers, we are watching an iconic moment in popular British culture. Along with *TW3*, a certain Phillip Larkin poem, the Beatles and the Profumo affair, the Cortina marked the end of the post-war consensus. Its predecessor, the Consul, together with the Standard Vanguard, stood for 1950s solidity. But in 1963, although it still bore the Consul prefix, the lightweight Cortina made most 1.5 litre British family cars appear lumpen and middle-aged – including Ford's own Classic.

Thus, Glamcabs offer sexual glamour and chromium trim against the BMC solidity of Speedee Cabs – the Cortinas all sport a love-heart shaped roof sign and are driven by Miss Barrie and co., who all seem to favour basques as part of their uniform. Speedee Cabs soon lose their male customers, apart from the camp Michael Ward, and Sid is forced to propose a merger with Glamcabs.

Learning for the first time the identity of 'Mrs. Glam' he storms off to seek solace in a whisky bottle. Obviously the male status quo must be resolved by the final reel, for this is a British family comedy of 1963 vintage. So, as soon as the audience sees a Glamcab being overtaken by a Mk2 Jaguar, they can work out the following sequence of events – hold up, Sid to the rescue, reconciliation. Cue theme music.

Nurse on Wheels

GB, 1963, 86mins, b&w

Dir: Gerald Thomas

Simper, simper, simper, or how to waste a talented actress in just 86 minutes. Juliet Mills fails to come to terms with the complicated controls of her Mini-Minor Super.

The Early Bird

GB, 1965, 90mins, colour

Dir: Robert Asher

The three Wisdom films in this section were chosen mainly for their automotive interests, together with the fact that they formed staple viewing for 1970s youth, be it in the surviving

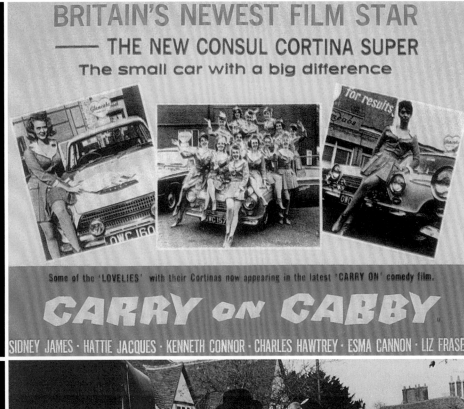

Publicity poster for *Carry On Cabby* showed how Ford capitalised on this early example of product placement with the new Cortina. *(Photo: Rank/ Pictorial Press Limited)*

Juliet Mills simpers at her crusty boss in pre-Germaine Greer comedy *Nurse on Wheels*. *(Photo: Anglo Amalgamated/GHW/ Pictorial Press Limited)*

Saturday cinema shows or on BBC1 Sunday matinees. As most of the world knows, in the vast bulk of Wisdom's 1950s films, our hero wore the Gump costume, knocked over costermongers' barrows and won the heart of the female lead. Furthermore, we shouldn't laugh at him 'cos he's a fool.

The Early Bird is Wisdom's first colour vehicle and the one in which he shouts 'Mr Grimsdale' a lot. Aside from causing a tree to fall on Jerry Desmonde's Bentley S2 (or what looks like a wooden dummy at the point of destruction), the chief motoring interest is noting the passage of time, even in Wisdom's realm.

Doctor in Clover
GB, 1966, 101mins, colour
Dir: Ralph Thomas

No 'Doctor' comedy from the Box/Thomas stable was complete without James Robertson-Justice being blustering and pompous in a pre-war Rolls-Royce. This has Leslie Phillips going 'mod' – avoid.

That Riviera Touch
GB, 1966, 98mins, colour
Dir: Cliff Owen

That Riviera Touch is the best of the three attempts to translate Morecambe and Wise onto the big screen; *The Intelligence Men* was studio bound (although it did feature a rather nice MkX with a Webasto roof) and a really uneven script plus Buckinghamshire doubling for Latin America defeated The Magnificent Two. But *Riviera* starts in a very promising fashion with Eric and Ernie as traffic wardens ticketing a Morris 1100. In fact, the only visible foreign model is a Fiat 2300 Familiare, but we digress. Eric then manages to book the Queen's Phantom V for having no licence plates whilst Ernie alternates between grovelling and hiding behind a Police Box. However, spending their savings on a holiday in the south of France should compensate for their instant resignation.

Unusually for a mid-1960s British comedy, *Riviera* did

Eric Morecambe and Ernie Wise inviting Suzanne Lloyd, the female interest in *That Riviera Touch*, to step aboard Eric's Mustang convertible. *(Photo: Rank Film Distributors Limited)*

Below, left to right: Sid James, Joan Sims, Bernard Bresslaw and Dilys Laye (in the back seat of the Ford Consul) in *Carry on Camping*. (Photo: Rank/Pictorial Press Limited)

Right: In *Let's Get Laid*, Robin Askwith and love interest get to know each other in the back of a Rolls-Royce. (Photo: Rank/Pictorial Press Limited)

include a fair amount of location footage and a thrilling car chase to boot. Morecambe and Wise drive a 1925 Bean – they are supposedly English eccentrics – but they become involved with a ruthless gem smuggler, the subtly named Le Pirate. As portrayed by Paul Stassino, a Maltese actor who seemed to forever play Middle-Eastern spies, Le Pirate wears an eye-patch and drives a Mercedes-Benz 190SL. Surely, a top international criminal would drive the latest Pagoda SL or even a classic Gullwing, but again one is forgetting the budgetary limitations. Likewise, Eric manages to win millions of francs at the lottery and decides to buy a Mustang convertible. 'It is like lightning Monsieur,' says the dealer, although if it is the six-cylinder model this is only in comparison with a Cortina GT.

The final two reels are devoted to the – obligatory – chase with Le Pirate's 190SL being pursued by both M and W in the Bean and the police in a black 1960 403 Berlina. This particular Peugeot should be familiar to ITC fans – it makes nearly as many appearances for Lew Grade as a certain Mk1 Jaguar driving over a cliff. Cliff Owen had previously directed *The Wrong Arm of the Law* and despite the back projection, he also stages a pretty gripping chase for M and W, with the police car nearly skidding over a precipice at one point. Eric and Ernie manage to drive their

car into the sea – a sequence forever appearing on BBC1's *Screen Test* – but naturally villainy doesn't triumph in a film that is a highly recommended way in which to spend a Saturday afternoon. It is the only M and W film that works as a narrative as opposed to an Eric and Ernie vehicle, the colour cinematography looks pin-sharp and expensive and there is even a break for Ernie to croon a very 1965 ballad à la Matt Monro. And, unlike Hope and Crosby or Martin and Lewis, they both get the girl.

Carry On Camping
GB, 1969, 88mins, colour
Dir: Gerald Thomas
Sid James and Bernard Breslaw persuade 'the girls' to go on a camping trip, taking Sid's Ford Consul MkII and, as usual, hoping for a leg-over. All characters are present in this film, probably the last half-watchable 'Carry On'.

Let's Get Laid
GB, 1978, 92mins, colour
Dir: James Kenelm Clarke
Robin Askwith sports a 1960s haircut and the set is dotted with 1950s cars. It must be a 1970s low-budget British comedy with a 1940s setting.

international comedy

mokes, mustangs, mini skirts and swinging london

Peter Sellers climbing into the
psychedelically painted Ford Country
Squire in *I Love You, Alice B. Toklas*.
(Photo: Warner/Seven Arts/
Pictorial Press Limited)

ANY YOUNGER READER who equates 1960s British
cinema with *Austin Powers* is in for a timely awakening.
Alfie (see 'Heroes and Villains') released in 1966 when that
decade was more than half over, owes a great deal to the
'kitchen sink' era which immediately preceded it – our anti-
hero being as much a 1950s relic as his E-Series Velox. Of
the two Richard Lester-directed Beatles films, *A Hard Day's
Night* has fleeting glimpses of MkIX Jaguars and Vanden
Plas Austin Princess limousines, while *Help!* features a
pursuit sequence, Bahamian Police Oxford Farinas and a
Minx Series III 1600. Similarly 1967's *Bedazzled*, one of the
most underrated and stylish British comedies of the late
1960s boasts no Mini Coopers or Mokes but instead a
Freestone & Webb-bodied Silver Cloud, plus an Armstrong-
Siddeley Sapphire 346 in a film that slyly implies the
involvement of Hell in Britain's post-war development.

So, we look towards those Hollywood-backed vehicles
for American stars 'right here in London'. This is the sub-
genre that seems to have made such an impression on
Mike Myers; the crane shots of red London buses driving
over Tower Bridge, the over-use of the words 'fab' and
'groovy' and the valiant efforts of the British supporting cast
to hide the vacuous nature of the entire enterprise. Certainly,
if any reader can voluntarily sit through *Kaleidoscope* ('The
Switched-on Thriller!') they must be rabid fans of either the
DB5 Volante or of Warren Beatty. *Arabesque* has Sophia
Loren in a fetching red Mercedes-Benz 250SL-mackintosh
ensemble, assassins in black MkIII Zephyr-Sixes, Gregory
Peck proving that Cary Grant is indeed inimitable and, best
of all, Alan Badel as the camp foot fetishist Arab villain.

In fact, on re-watching British films of this era, it is
striking how frequently American cars were still used as
symbols of decadent hipness, and some of the best use of
imported Yank tanks was by Michael Winner: the Buick
Riviera in 1964's *The System* and the Lincoln Continental in
You Must Be Joking in the following year. Both stand as
icons of unattainable luxury in slick and very well-observed
comedies. *Gonks Go Beat*, with its Ford Mustang, is ghastly

enough to merit a separate entry (see 'horror & fantasy'),
but more intriguing still is the pink 1962 Chevrolet Impala
driven by Harry Andrews in *Entertaining Mr Sloane*. For the
film's British viewers this would be the most accurate
replication of their own experience of North American cars;
several years out of date, quite possibly Canadian, featuring
the cheapest combination of a six-cylinder engine and a
manual column change, but still the hippest car in suburbia.

At a price of little over £2,000 the Jaguar E-type was an
accessible symbol of male success; it may have cost as
much as three Triumph Heralds but for a young professional
to dream of owning one was far more plausible than aiming
for £5,000-worth of Aston Martin. *Catch Us If You Can* is a
very early anti-Swinging London movie from 1965. Scripted
by Peter Nichols and directed by John Boorman it has
Barbara Ferris and Dave Clark taking off in an E-type to
escape from the media world only to find dead holiday
resorts and overweight beatniks.

The Mini-Moke, available as either an Austin or a Morris
according to your marque loyalty, cost less than £500 new
(sans passenger seats, heater, etc) boasted questionable
secondary safety features (largely nil) and was one of the
stars of *Blow-Up*. It continued to be used as a lethargic
form of visual shorthand in the death throes of the 1960s.
1968's *Salt and Pepper* boasts not only Sammy Davis Jr but
also a toupeed Peter Lawford as two hip night club owners
who pilot a customised and amphibious Mini-Moke; a film
that seems to prove the old adage that late-Swinging
London films seemed to be about 40-year-old men trying to
look 30 and score with 'chicks' aged 20.

Many of the best films of this era owe little or nothing to
the swinging myths spread via glossy magazines and
advertising copywriters. At their best they have an infectious
optimism – the hitch-hiking ride on the car-transporter full of
Cortina Aeroflows in *The Knack*; an emotional urgency –
consumer goods such as a Renault Carravelle failing to
stave off mental collapse in *The Pumpkin Eater*; or a wry wit
– Michael Crawford and Oliver Reed avoiding flotillas of

police 6/110s in *The Jokers*. As for the 3s 9d paying patrons of the Odeon or ABC, they may have marvelled at the mini-skirts and daring 3in sideburns on the screen but as they drove home in their Singer Gazelle their thoughts probably turned towards a nice tea of ham salad before *No Hiding Place* on the TV and a comforting mug of Horlicks.

The Absent-minded Professor

US, 1961, 97mins, b&w

Dir: Robert Stevenson

This Disney film is about professor Fred MacMurray's invention of 'flying rubber', which he calls 'flubber' and uses to power his family car to amazing effect (including mixing it in the sky with USAF jet fighters). There are those who would steal the secret from him, and so unfolds the story.

A Hard Day's Night/Help!

GB, 1964/65, 85mins/92mins, b&w/colour

Dir: Richard Lester

The most enduring vehicular image from *A Hard Day's Night* is the Beatles' black Austin Princess, not a prop but the actual car they used. It had a manual gearbox and Lennon called it their 'getaway car' because it sped them away from the clamouring crowds of girls. The memorable vehicle in *Help!* is a Hillman Minx 1600 saloon piloted by less-than-super villains Victor Spinetti and Roy Kinnear.

The Great Race

US, 1965, 111mins, colour

Dir: Blake Edwards

An indulgent but amusing romp from *Pink Panther* director Blake Edwards who teams-up with Jack Lemon (baddy in black hat) and Tony Curtis (goody in white suit) in this comedy about a 1908 New York to Paris race, loosely based on the real thing. It cost $8 million to make and featured specially constructed cars: Lemon's Hannibal 8 was an elevator car with a spiked nose cone powered by a Corvair engine. The Leslie special was built of PVC and designed to look like a real car of the period, the Thomas Flyer.

48

Fred MacMurray in a flubber-driven
vintage car flying alongside a USAF
Convair F102 Delta Dart all-weather
long-range interceptor in *The Absent-
minded Professor*.
(Photo: Disney/Pictorial Press Limited)

David Hemmings in his Silver Cloud being engaged by two hopeful models who are keen to have him photograph them David Bailey style in *Blow-Up*. *(Photo: MGM/Carlo Ponti/Pictorial Press Limited)*

Scoutmaster Terry-Thomas's overladen Boy Scouts Morris Mini-Moke attracts the attention of motorcycle cop Ian Hendry in a London street in *The Sandwich Man*. Hendry, one of the most under-rated actors of the '60s and '70s, in the '80s had a role in TV's *Brookside*. *(Photo: Pictorial Press Limited)*

Bob a job week

TITAN INTERNATIONAL presents
THE SANDWICH MA[N]
starring MICHAEL BENTINE · DORA BRYAN
HARRY H. CORBETT · BERNARD CRIBBINS
DIANA DORS · IAN HENDRY · STANLEY HOLLOW[AY]
WILFRID HYDE-WHITE · MICHAEL MEDWI[N]
RON MOODY · ANNA QUAYLE · TERRY-THOM[AS]
NORMAN WISDOM · DONALD WOLFIT
IN COLOUR
DISTRIBUTED BY THE RANK ORGANISATION

The Knack... and How to Get It

GB, 1965, 84mins, b&w

Dir: Richard Lester

Ray Brooks (Tolen) as the epitome of suburban cool on his Triumph motorcycle with Jane Birkin on the pillion seat. Yes, but then when one takes in Mr Tolen's teddy-boy quiff and black suit, then it is obvious that his downfall – being trampled underfoot by mini-skirted extras emerging from a Morris Mini – is inevitable, for Tolen is merely another suburban square.

Blow-Up

GB, 1966, 110mins, colour

Dir: Michelangelo Antonioni

Antonioni's Marxist concerns transposed to swinging London, following the existential odyssey of hip photographer and ex-Children's Film Foundation star David Hemmings driving a fabulous black 'Chinese eye' Rolls-Royce Silver Cloud drophead through the capital. The car, formerly white and originally owned by Jimmy Saville, was fitted with a radio phone. The film's commercial success was quite immense, although the cynical may apportion some of it to brief full-frontal female nudity – this, of course, is quite acceptable in an art movie.

Kaleidoscope

GB, 1966, 103mins, colour

Dir: Jack Smight

Warren Beatty, being a swinging hip kind of guy, drives a DB5 convertible in this story of an American playboy who breaks into a playing card factory and alters the designs so he can win in the European casinos using some special glasses. Very much the same vein as *Arabesque* though a lot more watchable. To really push home the fact that the action takes place in 'swinging' England, the baddy, as usual, drives a Silver Cloud – in this case a Cloud III in white which Eric Porter – international criminal of the cravat and cigarette holder school – uses to chase Mr Beatty and his leading lady Susannah York down a tunnel (as pedestrians)

at the same time asking his chauffeur what the horsepower of the Cloud is. 'About 200 Sir,' he replies – a pretty fair guess, as R-R didn't reveal bhp figures in those days.

The Sandwich Man

GB, 1966, 95mins, colour

Dir: Robert Hartford-Davis

Michael Bentine, the fourth member of *The Goon Show*, made very few film appearances, chiefly concentrating on his stage and well-remembered children's TV programmes. *The Sandwich Man* was his only starring cinema vehicle and, in the truly biased view of this writer, is an utterly beguiling combination of Jacques Tati and Swinging London.

The eponymous central character, one Horace Quimby, wanders throughout the city observing, but rarely partaking in, the Bentine-devised visual gags: Scoutmaster Terry-Thomas knocks speed-cop Ian Hendry off his Triumph in his attempts to load an over-sized back-pack onto a Morris Mini-Moke whilst two Australians, both dressed as kangaroos for an advertising promotion, crash their MkIII Zephyr-Sixes and start thumping each other. At the film's climax, Horace and co. take a ride along the Thames in a white Amphicar in a sequence that should have done (but didn't) for the Amphicar what *Carry On Cabby* did for the Mk1 Cortina.

Casino Royale

GB, 1967, 131mins, colour

Dir: Val Guest, Joe McGrath, John Huston, Ken Hughes, Robert Parrish

If *Casino Royale* were a car it would be a 1967 Vauxhall Viscount, in burgundy. For my *raison d'être* behind this outrageous slur, read on.

The story behind the sorry mess is well enough known; the 007 spoofs had reached their zenith by 1965–66 and there were supposedly sufficient punters who were deluded enough to believe in Swinging London to make production of a groovy faux-Bond film worthwhile. Furthermore, the producer Charles Feldman owned the rights to Fleming's novel but was unable to prise Mr Connery away from Messrs Saltzman and Broccoli. So, why not pack the narrative with hip and with-it stars? Nearly two hours of running time is a terribly long period to discover exactly why not. And yet it all begins in such promising vein – from an automotive point of view that is. Just after the Herb Alpert theme music has faded, we see a Citroën DS Pallas, a Cadillac Fleetwood, a Volga M22 and a Daimler DR450 (the last true Daimler) arrive at the gates of a baronial pile in Scotland.

The DR450 should be particularly familiar to *The Italian Job* fans; it plays the part of the Pakistani High Commissioner's stolen limousine. It transpires that these black and official looking vehicles belong to the respective heads of the Deuxieme Bureau, the CIA, the KGB and MI5 and that all of these spymasters have come to lure Sir James Bond out of retirement. Sir James, as it transpires, is decidedly miffed about his celluloid doppelganger – 'An Aston Martin complete with lethal accessories,' he sniffs – so there will be no gadget-laden transport for David Niven. In fact, after the first reel there is not all that much to entertain the motor enthusiast, and it is not as if the plot doesn't allow for some gripping chases.

There is one fairly lengthy car chase; albeit one that would not give Peter Yates insomnia. Escaping from Scotland, and John Huston's truly leaden comedy direction, Sir James is pursued by Gabrielle Licudi (of the cult British sci-fi classic *Unearthly Stranger*) in her canary yellow Series One E-type roadster. Naturally, Gabrielle, clad in her best Carnaby Street rags, is working for SMERSH and we cut to a control room staffed by black-jump-suited Amazons with Roedean accents. The head Amazon sets in motion their deadly weapon – a remote control 1962 Bedford CA Milkfloat (DRINKA PINTA MILKA DAY) equipped with battering rams and other devices not approved by the Milk Marketing Board. The chase is now in earnest with lots of matte shots, footage of Ireland doubling for Scotland, and shots of the Amazons monitoring the pursuit on their Scalextrix track (!). Of course, an Italian starlet is no match

for David Niven in a BRG Bentley 3-litre and the chase ends with a completely gratuitous shot of Gabrielle being pronged by the Bedford. End of chase and we are still more than an hour from the final credits.

After this point, there is very little of interest for the motor enthusiast; Inspector Duncan Macrae has a very nice DS21 as his staff car, but this is the one exception to a litany of missed opportunities. In the novel, Le Chiffre drove a grey Traction Avant, so where was its 1967 equivalent, for Orson Welles deserved at least a DS Prestige or even an FV Excellance? This is also one of the few Swinging London films sans Mini-Moke. Maybe they were all spoken for by Antonioni and Patrick McGoohan.

I Love You, Alice B. Toklas
US, 1968, 93mins, colour
Dir: Hy Averback

There's a reasonable theory that Peter Sellers's authority as a screen actor declined in equal measure as his taste in cars became ever more grandiose and it will take something more than a Ford Country Squire painted psychedelic colours to make him a swinging kind of guy once more.

The Brain
Fr/US, 1969, 115mins, colour
Dir: Gérard Oury

The Brain is the story of an English Colonel who leads a robbery attempt on NATO. Jean Paul Belmondo provides the swarthy euro-hunk interest (it was a joint French/US production) and does a lot of leaping about, while David Niven, following from his triumphs in *Casino Royale*, looks like a piece of chipboard throughout most of this breathless, glossy international crook caper, but it's worth watching for the stunt where the Citroën DS is chopped in half (repeated with a Renault 11 in *A View to a Kill* in the mid-'80s) and for some early scenes involving a BMW 2000CS Coupé in orange speeding through the streets of Paris. The near obligatory Swinging London scenes in the first reel boast police S-types and 6/110s.

The ultimate cut'n'shut Citroën DS that features in *The Brain*. Bourvil seems to share critics' opinion of the film. *(Photo: Paramount/Pictorial Press Limited)*

Michael Caine finishes off what the JCB started on this very early E-type Coupé in *The Italian Job* as the crew look on.
(Photo: Paramount/Oakhurst/BFI)

Below: This scene, where the Minis do a highly choreographed waltz with the Police Alfas, was cut from the film on the grounds of self-indulgence, probably quite rightly.
(Photo: Paramount/Oakhurst/BFI)

Opposite top: Mini-Coopers in *The Italian Job* descend the carpeted staircase of one of Turin's historic buildings.
(Photo: Paramount/Oakhurst/Pictorial Press Limited)

Opposite bottom: Two of the gold-laden Mini-Coopers rendezvous with the getaway coach in *The Italian Job*, one making its bid to climb the trailing ramps.
(Photo: Paramount/Oakhurst/Pictorial Press Limited)

The Italian Job

GB, 1969, 96mins, colour
Dir: Peter Collinson

The Italian Job is a film that certain sections of the British media herald as exemplifying the New Lad form of protracted adolescence – British cars and a (mainly) British cast stealing Italian gold whilst singing jolly geezers songs and being dressed as football supporters in an era when the words 'British' and 'football' still held fresh memories of 1966 and didn't put the entire Carabinieri on full alert. It stars Michael Caine, the embodiment of the working-class lad made good, and the Austin Mini-Cooper S, the car that won the Monte Carlo Rally three times (discounting the rulings of the untrustworthy French in 1966). Alternatively, it is a British crime-caper film in the tradition of *The Lavender Hill Mob* and *The Wrong Arm of the Law*, boasting Douglas Slocombe's colour cinematography and foreign location footage at the expense of a cohesive narrative; instead relying on impressive performances and very elaborate set pieces.

In fact the narrative can be quite easily bisected – the first four/five reels detail the Ealing comedy type antics of an over-confident would-be master criminal and his hand-picked inept gang, the remainder being given over to the real *raison d'être* – the chase sequence, for without the pursuit the film may as well have stayed in London amongst the Met's S-types and 6/110s. The plot proper begins with Rossano Brazzi – whom we last saw crashing a Lamborghini Muira into a JCB after the opening credits – selling Charlie a plan to rob the city of Turin of a $4 million consignment of gold. To carry out this plan, Charlie seeks the financial aid of Mr Bridger (Noel Coward) who runs Britain's underworld from his gaol cell and also considers Charlie to be moderately incompetent. Even after the funding is eventually given, the gang seem to specialise in crashing Mini-Coopers and demolishing bullion vans. Charlie at least knows the virtue of putting on a good front, favouring a silver DB4 Volante as his personal transport in contrast to 'The Heavies' – familiar from about every British crime film made in the '50s and '60s – who still use a Ford Thames Van, a vehicle fitted with one of Britain's most dreadful column shifts, rather than the latest in Transits. As always, it is these incidental details that date the film, along with the 'chicks' in their M&S undergarments and the nominal female lead who has virtually nothing to do. Anyway, after a funeral scene (shot in Eire because of Noel Coward's tax status) and with a Daimler DR450 making a cameo appearance, the action shifts to the Continent and things begin to pick up pace, particularly for Euro-Box spotters. It is also at this point in the film that certain problems in the script begin to surface. It has often been stated that Troy Kennedy Martin's original screenplay was intended as a light satire of the English abroad, and whilst elements of this still work – Charlie blithely warning his troops that the Italians drive 'on the wrong side of the road' – the first meeting of Charlie and Altabani still lingers unpleasantly in the memory.

Yes, the Mafia have destroyed the DB4 (actually a mocked-up Alfa Romeo 2000 Spyder) plus two E-type 3.8 Coupés, but Charlie's invocation of reprisals against England's entire Italian community now appears less than hilarious – Powellite politics not being known for their lightness of touch.

The film has equal appeal for both owners of Mini-Coopers (all privately bought because BMC were not interested in supplying them) and Italian car enthusiasts, the latter inevitably annoyed at the lazy film journalists still perpetuating the old chestnut that Fiat rather magnanimously provided the police cars. As every motoring enthusiast knows, they were all Alfa Romeo Giulia TI saloons, and there's really little excuse for making such a crass mistake.

Given the use of Fiat's own factory in Turin, it is obvious that their products would dominate the location footage. Most of them would have been not unfamiliar to the British audience at the time – Fiat was the only car importer to boast a line-up as comprehensive as that of Austin or Vauxhall – and the street scenes are littered with the 500s,

600s, 850s 1100Rs plus the 1300/1500s and their successor the 124, a car sadly besmirched by its unfortunate USSR connotations. Sightings of the majestically be-finned 2300 saloon are less common and Lancia enthusiasts will wince at the appearance of a heavily dented Flaminia Coupé. There's even the odd British import, such as a well-used Consul Classic saloon, finished in maroon no less. But of all the Fiats in the street scenes, nothing could compare with Raf Vallone's flotilla of Dino Coupés.

The colour photography shows the red, white and blue Coopers to the best advantage as they career along Turin's piazzas and through tunnels (actually shot in Coventry). The scene with the Bedford coach is utterly ingenious (although not without antecedents – *Robbery* and *The League of Gentlemen*) and the whole film has just about enough charm to overcome its more dated elements and to make one wish to snatch it from the jaws of film cultists. And then there's the final scene, consciously or unconsciously encapsulating the state not only of the Britain's film industry, as the Americans prepared to decamp, but of her motor industry and even her national identity. *The Italian Job* was one of the last films to display such jaunty self-confidence in British products with a British leading man for nearly a decade.

Monte Carlo or Bust!
(aka Those Daring Young Men in Their Jaunty Jalopies)
GB/It/Fr, 1969, 119mins, colour
Dir: Ken Annakin

If Annakin's *The Fast Lady* was sharp, witty and concise, then this film is merely overblown. Not even a cast that included Tony Curtis, Terry-Thomas, Eric Sykes, Jack Hawkins and Pete and Dud could rescue this indulgent, overlong vintage car romp set in the '20s, that was really an earthbound version of *Those Magnificent Men in Their Flying Machines*, but it's probably worth watching for the genuine vintage cars – Lancia Lambda among them – and the expensive looking period detail.

A publicity poster for 1969's *Monte Carlo or Bust!* (Photo: Paramount/Dino de Laurentis/Marianne)

PARAMOUNT PICTURES
PRESENTS
KEN ANNAKIN'S
PRODUCTION OF

MONTE CARLO OR BUST!

A RACE FOR GLORY, FOR LOVE AND FOR THE FUN OF IT!

STARRING (IN ALPHABETICAL ORDER)
BOURVIL ⊙ LANDO BUZZANCA ⊙ WALTER CHIARI ⊙ PETER COOK ⊙ TONY CURTIS ⊙ MIREILLE DARC ⊙ MARIE DUBOIS ⊙ GERT FROBE
SUSAN HAMPSHIRE ⊙ JACK HAWKINS ⊙ NICOLETTA MACHIAVELLI ⊙ DUDLEY MOORE ⊙ PEER SCHMIDT ⊙ ERIC SYKES ⊙ TERRY-THOMAS
PRODUCED AND DIRECTED BY KEN ANNAKIN ⊙ ORIGINAL STORY AND SCREENPLAY BY JACK DAVIES AND KEN ANNAKIN ⊙ ASSOCIATE PRODUCER BASIL KEYS
TITLE SONG, MUSIC AND LYRIC BY RON GOODWIN—SUNG BY JIMMY DURANTE, AND OTHER MUSIC FROM THE MOTION PICTURE SCORE AVAILABLE ON PARAMOUNT RECORDS ⊙ TECHNICOLOR* ⊙ PANAVISION ⊙ A PARAMOUNT PICTURE

The System

GB, 1964, 90mins, b&w

Dir: Michael Winner

'What do you want, her or the Riviera?' Reed: 'Either.' A Buick Riviera stars alongside Oliver Reed in this stylish little tale about seaside yobs chasing rich crumpet. Oliver Reed, who in real life drove a Panther Royale in the 1970s when he was sober enough to take the wheel, was a favourite actor of director Michael Winner. He featured in Winner's 1967 *I'll Never Forget Whatsisname* (the first British film ever to use the 'F' word) driving an Alfa Romeo 2600 Spider.

There's a Girl in My Soup

GB, 1970, 96mins, colour

Dir: Roy Boulting

Peter Sellers's taste in cars is reflected in this screen version of the stage play, also starring Goldie Hawn. Actually, the 'Chinese eye' Silver Cloud III drophead and even rarer 'adaptation' Silver Cloud III drophead (using the saloon styling) were both quite old cars by the time this glossy, uninspiring film was made – a far cry from *I'm All Right Jack*. Peter Sellers changed his cars as regularly as his socks. Anthony Crook, the managing director of Bristol Cars Ltd, did all the star's car dealing in the 1960s but, curiously, Sellers never actually owned a Bristol.

What's Up, Doc?

US, 1972, 94mins, colour

Dir: Peter Bogdanovich

Ryan O'Neal pretends to be frightened either by Barbra Streisand's driving or perhaps her ego. In the film, the Beetle is very obviously stunt-driven.

No Deposit, No Return

US, 1976, 112mins, colour

Dir: Norman Tokar

Despite the car chase this is just more proof that Disney should stick to cartoons. You'll probably recognise this sequence from *Screen Test* or *Clapper Board*, the children's Cinema magazine programmes of 1970s British TV.

Ferris Bueller's Day Off

US, 1986, 103mins, colour

Dir: John Hughes

This '80s teenage comedy had its moments but sadly the Ferrari 250 Californian Spider at the centre of the farce was a glass fibre, Corvette-powered, fake which now hangs in a Planet Hollywood restaurant in Minnesota.

Below: Ryan O'Neal covers his eyes at Barbra Streisand's ineptitude at the wheel of her Beetle in *What's Up, Doc?* (Photo: Warner/Saticoy/Pictorial Press Limited)

Bottom: The fake Ferrari in *Ferris Bueller's Day Off*. (Photo: Paramount/John Hughes/Pictorial Press Limited)

Teetering on the brink after a disastrous car chase in *No Deposit, No Return* are two of the most inefficient detectives in the business. *(Photo: Disney/Pictorial Press Limited)*

horror & fantasy

sinister, satanic and science fiction

FANTASY CINEMA CAN MEAN Sgt. Edward Woodward's Mini Panda Car in *The Wicker Man* or the twin E-types of *Mr Diabolik*, cannibalistic Renault R8 drivers in *Weekend*, zombies in a respectable Hillman-driving 1950s New Zealand in *Braindead* or Bentley S2 driving maniacs in *Stop Me Before I Kill!* If the reader finds this chapter dominated by films from Bray Studios and their ilk, we apologise but would merely like to observe that when excess and restraint collide in the cinema, post-war British fantasy films have no equal.

Viewers of the amiable comedy *Back to the Future Part II* must have noticed that one of the taxi-cabs circa 2015 was a Citroën DS. This is a true testament to the Citroën's styling which implies modernist optimism as much as the De Lorean signifies industrial inertia. The black P6 Rovers in *Gattaca* seem to perform a similar function to the narrative, with the added advantage that they would be virtually unknown to a young American audience circa 1997.

So, when setting a story in the future, the film-maker has several options. The first is to use contemporary cars imaginatively – such as in *Alphaville* and the Zephyr-Six MkIV Farnham in *No Blade of Grass*. The second is to construct vehicles to reflect the narrative's apocalyptic/dystopian/optimistic viewpoint. A third is to use contemporary vehicles and hope that no-one will notice the heroes making a getaway in a 200 year old Morris-Commercial – see *Daleks Invasion Earth 2150 AD*. Finally, there are those celluloid narratives set in a time and place that bear a passing resemblance to a bygone era. The Morris Minors and Oxford M.O.s in *The Borrowers* are right-hand drive (but drive on the right) and reinforce the film's vaguely 1950s atmosphere.

Try to imagine *Duel* if the oil-tanker in it was the latest 1971 model or that Dennis Weaver's character was a middle-aged farmer in a clapped-out Oldsmobile 88. *Duel*'s scenario needs Spielberg's lower-middle-class figure of neutered masculinity in a mundane Valiant as much as the oil-tanker needs to be antiquated and begrimed.

A gifted film-maker can imbue the most mundane and dreary of cars with varying degrees of menace, angst and rage. Polanski's use of the Morris Minor in *Cul-de-Sac* is dealt with separately, but see how Jean-Luc Godard uses Simca 1500 police cars in his totalitarian fantasy *Alphaville* or how the humble 2CV, a familiar and jolly presence in innumerable French comedies, is the harbinger of doom in *Les Diaboliques* and *Les Yeux Sans Visage*. Equally naturally, film-makers who seem to lack either the budget, talent or cast, also try to use standard cars as totems of evil and totally fail to keep bathos at bay. *The Psychopath* features various chaps being run over by a solidly bourgeois Volvo 122S whilst *The Crucible of Terror* features the twin threats of Mike Raven's acting and a Ford Escort Mk1.

Crash should be a uniquely troubling film but I found it pedestrian. Also, it was a criminal waste of both a Lincoln Continental convertible and Holly Hunter. There are far more shocking moments involving motor accidents in films of a far lesser budget. The well-regarded British sci-fi B-film *Invasion* has one of the main characters dying horribly as his Oxford VI Traveller crashes into a force-field. Up until this point, the film had been a low-key evocation of rural England under siege, so the timing of the crash was as significant as its execution. However, largely because of budget limitations, the horror/fantasy genre seems to include more totally pathetic car crashes than virtually any other genre. The first ever Amicus Film, *Dr Terror's House of Horrors* has Christopher Lee driving his Rover 75 Cyclops whilst being strangled by Michael Gough's disembodied hand, a scene only bettered by the awesomely weedy scene of Edward Judd's Daimler Sovereign crashing into a tree in *The Vault of Horror*.

On first sight of the young couple in *Night of the Living Dead*, the average viewer knows that some terrible fate is about to befall them; they're young, totally square and drive a conservatively fast Pontiac. They probably voted for Nixon too. Romero's 1968 film arguably had as great an impact on the genre as did the first Hammer Horrors a decade earlier, not least for the *Living Dead*'s evocation of a

Shall we dance? Evil Lincoln-based car threatens Z-movie actors in *The Car*. (Photo: Universal/Pictorial Press Limited)

decaying contemporary society, as opposed to the floridly coloured fantasy land of Hammer. In fact Hammer's output was not restricted to gothic horror, and certainly Val Guest's two *Quatermass* films of the 1950s combine genuine location footage and heroes in everyday vehicles – Austin 16s, Humber Hawk MkIV estate cars – to good paranoid effect. His best film in the sci-fi genre was *The Day the Earth Caught Fire*, not least for the scene in which Edward Judd's Morris Minor is flagged down by the future Sir Maurice Micklewhite in yet another of his many bit parts.

So, although the cars in *The Devil Rides Out* are splendid it still falls into the Hammer-Gothic category, but there's always 1966's *The Witches*. Joan Fontaine drives a Riley Elf III (with winding windows no less) as befitting her status as the village's new headmistress. Unfortunately the entire Women's Institute seem to be practising witchcraft, but at least Miss Fontaine drives a car with leather upholstery, so it's not such a bad career move. Meanwhile, in 1969's *The Haunted House of Horror*, George Sewell drives a MkIV Zodiac so his early demise is inevitable – had he chosen a Rover 2000TC or a Triumph 2.5 PI he might have even survived until the final reel. Better still is *Earth Dies Screaming* in which alien robots are despatched by being run over by a Land Rover, and angry young men steal PB-Series Crestas. By the early 1970s, spurred on by *Night of The Living Dead*, even Hammer had started to give *Count Dracula* a contemporary setting with Triumph Stags in *Dracula AD 1972* and P5B saloons in *The Satanic Rites of Dracula*, but for true horror nothing could equate with 1973's *Holiday on the Buses*. It even has Marinas in the background.

The Day the Earth Caught Fire

GB, 1961, 98mins, b&w
Dir: Val Guest

Moderately superior British sci-fi with Edward Judd (think once, think twice, think bike!) running around sweating a lot and driving a Morris Minor. Look out for the young Michael Caine and his two lines of dialogue as a copper.

The Birds

US, 1963, 119mins, colour
Dir: Alfred Hitchcock

Tippi Hedren uses an Aston Martin DB MkIII convertible throughout this allegorical Hitchcock piece about a flock of crows that attack people on an island for no apparent reason. The Aston looks, and sounds, classy among the random yankmobiles. Hitchcock liked to give his leading players up-market Euro machinery to give them a posh image. Remember the MkVIII Jaguar in *Vertigo*, and the Mercedes 220 Cabriolet in *North by Northwest*.

Night Must Fall

GB, 1964, 104mins, b&w
Dir: Karel Reisz

Despite a distinguished cast and director, this remake of the 1937 Hollywood original was not warmly received, but provides a view of Albert Finney driving a rare convertible Austin Mini built by Crayford Conversions of Kent.

Gonks Go Beat

GB, 1965, 90mins, b&w
Dir: Robert Hartford-Davis

In the future, planet earth is ruled by the two warring nations of Ballad Isle and Beat-Land. Only the intervention of Intergalactic Ambassador 'Wilco Roger' (Kenneth Connor) and 'Mr A&R' (Frank 'Captain Peacock' Thornton) can save the day. But this is more than a mere excuse for a really bizarre assortment of mid-'60s pop stars to mime to their greatest hits. No, *Gonks* also celebrates Britain's finest sports cars with a sequence in which a Sprite, Alpine III, MGB, Healey 3000, Spitfire and Galaxie 500 drophead career across the sands of 'Beat Land'. Unlike the two best-known Hartford-Davis films, *Saturday Night Out* and *The Sandwich Man* (q.v.), *Gonks Go Beat* surfaces on UK television but rarely. This is almost certainly a relief to the lemon-meringue quiffed Ballad Isle folk singer 'Derek' who bears a certain resemblance to both a BBC TV hospital soap nurse and Bob Hoskins's disloyal 2i/c from *The Long Good Friday*.

Edward Judd's split screen Minor
about to be overturned by trad jazz-
crazed Beatniks in Val Guest's *The
Day the Earth Caught Fire*.
*(Photo: British Lion/Pax/Pictorial Press
Limited)*

Flora Robson and a chaired Gig Young in front of the Thunderbird in *The Shuttered Room*.
(Photo: Warner/Troy/Schenck/ Pictorial Press Limited)

The Lancia Lambda used in the film *The Devil Rides Out*, with the Bentley showing alongside it. The driver is Jack Silk. Photo from his collection.

SEVEN ARTS PRODUCTIONS PRESENTS
"THE SHUTTERED ROOM"
starring
GIG YOUNG   CAROL LYNLEY
OLIVER REED   FLORA ROBSON
IN COLOUR
A TROY SCHENCK PRODUCTION   RELEASED BY WARNER PATHÉ

Cul-de-Sac

GB, 1966, 111mins, b&w

Dir: Roman Polanski

It takes a film-maker of Roman Polanski's calibre to highlight the macabre qualities within the humble Morris Minor Series 2, especially as this particular Morris is an L-Driver car commandeered by wounded gangster Albie (Jack MacGowran) and his American partner Dickie (HUAC victim Lionel Stander). Our first glimpse of the trio is of Stander pushing the Minor towards Lindisfarne Castle, where they hope to evade the law. But the tide is coming in fast across the causeway, threatening to completely submerge the 'Popular School of Motoring' Minor – 'In the shit thanks to your idiotic ideas,' grumbles Albie; and Dickie heads towards the castle to dragoon some help. Unfortunately, for Dickie, he has entered a realm that could have been devised by collaboration between Beckett and Pinter. The castle is occupied by a beautiful young Frenchwoman (Françoise Dorléac) and her totally bald upper-class English husband Donald Pleasence. Mr Pleasence is attired in a nightdress.

To describe the rest of the film would be to ruin the experience for any new viewer. Suffice to say that people have their feet set on fire, their bottoms spanked plus polo-necked William Franklyn turning up in a white MkX Jaguar, being mistaken for gang boss 'Fat Tony' and trying to flee across the sands in the MkX. The Jaguar is subsequently blown up by Lionel in a final gesture of futile machismo.

The Shuttered Room

GB, 1967, 110mins, colour

Dir: David Greene

We are expected to believe somewhere in Norfolk is an island off the New England coast in this Oliver Reed vehicle. The cast of mostly British character actors is another giveaway. But it's worth watching for the gold 1966 Thunderbird that careers along dusty roads at high speed, wallowing through corners and generally looking on the edge of control most of the time.

The Devil Rides Out

UK, 1968, 95mins, colour

Dir: Terence Fisher

One of the better Hammer efforts based on a Dennis Wheatley novel and set in the '20s. Veteran horror director Terence Fisher tried hard with the period detail, obtaining a Lancia Lambda and a Bentley 3-litre for a good chase sequence. The cars were supplied by the stuntman Jack Silk. 'It was a film that was always in trouble,' he says. 'The camera would stop working. The actor was sick. The cars got dents where they should never have had them. It was an unlucky car, the Lancia. They wanted to do a shot of the car drifting around a bend with correcting lock on. They mounted a camera on the running board, and half way round the drifting corner the front suspension came undone …' *EastEnders* fans can try to spot stunt man Mike Reid.

The Man Who Haunted Himself

GB, 1970, 89mins, colour

Dir: Basil Dearden

The Man Who Haunted Himself, made in 1970, was the first film Roger Moore made after finishing *The Saint*. He was keen to move away from the Simon Templar TV character and get into cinema released films, although he hadn't given up on the small screen: *The Persuaders* was still in the planning stages at around this time.

Essentially *The Man Who Haunted Himself* was a 'psychological thriller' about a boring businessman – Harold Pelham – who has a car crash and 'dies' momentarily on the operating table. At the moment of death his more exciting alter-ego takes on a life of its own and goes around the place doing things the boring Pelham would never dream of: pulling dolly birds, buying flash designer suits, gambling, getting pissed, buying Italian supercars, becoming embroiled in industrial espionage and generally having a good time.

Anyway, enough plot. This film is worth watching for the crash scene at the start. Pelham's car is a mulberry-coloured Rover 3.5-litre saloon – the Harold Wilson ministerial V8 barge of the period – which he drives ever so carefully at all times. Although not correct geographically, the title sequence sets the scene, showing Pelham driving from his offices on Millbank, along the embankment through Parliament Square (sad people will be on the pause button at this point to check up on '60s/'70s cars they'd almost forgotten about) and up onto the Hammersmith flyover (we are never told where he lives but you assume it's somewhere like Chiswick or Richmond). All this to a soundtrack of cheesy '70s easy listening.

We see the Rover driving gently along the elevated section of the M4, the anal Pelham observing the speed limit. Suddenly, he starts to sweat and pull at his clothes. Grinning demonically he removes his seat belt, grips the big plastic steering wheel and nails the throttle to the floor. 70, 80, 90mph: we get a close-up of the speedo needle surging round the dial (at a pace no 3.5 could ever achieve) as the car weaves its way through the traffic on the M4, crossplys screeching as the huge, wallowy saloon lurches from lane-to-lane. Pelham's devilish alter ego begins to emerge as the car sweeps up to 100mph, cutting up the other traffic – we keep seeing the same brown Mercedes 250SE saloon and a Sunbeam Alpine being almost pushed off the road.

Just as the driver has an alter ego, then so does the car: as the sweat beads gather on Pelham's forehead the Rover begins to morph into a different machine – something low and exciting to symbolise the driver's new personality.

Enter a silver Lamborghini Islero: cut to a shot of its headlamps popping up and Pelham aggressively snatching at the gears in one of those completely obvious studio shots that were the trademark of anything ITC produced.

Of course, it's all in his head, poor dear. The next thing Pelham sees is some roadworks. He tries to take avoidance measures but the Rover is doing three figures. He locks everything up and slews the car into a ludicrous spin that seems to go on forever, crashing into oil drums (what were they doing on the M4?) barriers and cones before coming to an abrupt halt, although you don't quite see the moment of impact. Later Pelham buys a new Rover – same colour,

same model (in fact, probably the same car but with a different number plate). His wife, exasperated by his predictability, asks, 'Why did you have to buy the same type of car again darling?', to which Rog' replies, 'Didn't see the point in changing. Damn fine motorcar.'

Duel
US, 1971, 90mins, colour
Dir: Steven Spielberg
Originally made for American TV, *Duel* was the film that made Speilberg's name as a director. Dennis Weaver (from the TV series *McCloud*) is an unassuming travelling salesman driving a Plymouth Valiant. For no apparent reason the driver of an 18-wheeler Kenworth rig takes against Mr Weaver and pursues him across desert terrain in a game of cat and mouse. We never see the driver of the Kenworth, only his cowboy boots and manly hands on the controls, and it is interesting that the truck easily out-performs the weedy straight-six Plymouth. This was released in the UK in 1972 but didn't make it to US cinemas until 1983 once Mr Spielberg was a household name.

Psychomania
GB, 1971, 95mins, colour
Dir: Don Sharp
This film proudly stands alongside *Beat Girl*, *The Singer Not the Song* and *Devil Girl from Mars* as a truly deranged British movie. The 'Living Dead' motorcycle gang is lead by aristocratic Nicky Henson, a rather strange young man who would rather collect frogs and lurk around the Seven Witches standing stones than cavort with his girlfriend Abby. What could be the reason for this. Is it the pressure of being a juvenile delinquent when your 30th birthday draws ever closer? Is it the disappointment of riding a second-hand AJS because the budget wouldn't run to Harley-Davidsons? But Nicky is a questing young man: 'Why did my father die in the locked room? Why do you never get any older? And what is the secret of the living dead?' Thus, he learns that mummy (Beryl Reid) is a medium and her butler Shadwell (George

Roger Moore at the wheel with Hildegarde Niel at his side in *The Man Who Haunted Himself*. *(Photo: Tribune/BFI Stills, Posters and Designs)*

Dennis Weaver making a run for his Plymouth Valiant at a desert petrol station in *Duel*. *(Photo: Universal/ Pictorial Press Limited)*

Sanders) is an emissary from Hell. Through a splendidly cheap flashback sequence we also discover that Nicky has been promised to old Nick at the Seven Witches and that one supposed fringe benefit is being able to survive death as an invincible zombie. Refreshed by this knowledge, Nicky leads the Living Dead on a rampage through the Hemel Hempstead branch of Fine Fare. The police are summoned in their white S-type and here the viewer can learn how a director can gain the maximum value from a limited amount of footage as we see the police car overtake the same black A40 Farina a mere ten times. The gang escape, but Chief Inspector Robert Hardy in his '69 P6 3500 is suspicious. Equally suspicious is Hardy's accent – why is a Bulgarian serving as a senior CID officer? – until one realises that this is the Hardy interpretation of a Brummagem plod.

But for sheer straight-faced comedy, *Psychomania* is Don Sharp's finest hour. Sharp specialised in splendid chase sequences – he directed much of *Those Magnificent Men in Their Flying Machines* plus the under-valued film version of *Callan* (q.v.) – but some film writers such as Steve Chibnall regard *Psychomania* as his greatest achievement, even if Nicky Henson has been reported to have complained that any time he takes on a major stage or TV role, the BBC schedule his finest hour just to haunt him.

Death Race 2000
US, 1975, 79mins, colour
Dir: Paul Bartel

A cross between *Rollerball* and *Wacky Races*, this black comedy is about a futuristic transcontinental race where contestants gain points by running over and killing pedestrians: pensioners and babies are worth the most points. Popular favourite Frankenstein (David Carradine) has had numerous limb transplants because of his previous crashes, and is now partially bionic. His car looks like a large fanged Godzilla head. 'Machine Gun' Joe Viterbo (Sylvester Stallone) is a gangster who sprays his machine gun into the stands before the race, jealous of the fans' adulation of Frankenstein. Calamity Jane Kelly (Mary

Woronov) is a cowgirl, and her car, 'The Bull', has dark brown spots and horns. Mathilda the Hun races with her navigator Herman the German in the 'Buzz Bomb'. Mathilda wears swastika armbands and a Nazi uniform. Ray Nero the Hero's ensemble has an Ancient Greek theme, along with his navigator Cleopatra. Their vehicle, the 'Lion' is gold and also features large fangs. Cleopatra, the navigator, feeds Ray grapes before the race.

The first kill on the race is made by 'Machine Gun' Joe, who bags a road worker. The deceased man's wife wins several prizes. Bartel's dark humour is obvious in many of the deaths of the pedestrians. Jane's first pedestrian is a bullfighter who tries to fight her car. Frankenstein kills several invalids (anyone over 70 is worth 100 points, the highest) who have been put in the middle of the road for 'Euthanasia Day' at the hospital. The plot revolves around a resistance group trying to end the violent race (Frankenstein's new navigator, Annie, is actually a spy for the resistance) as the various competitors are bumped-off.

The Car
US, 1977, 98mins, colour
Dir: Elliot Silverstein

Terrible film about a sinister black car, apparently driverless and possessed by the Devil, that terrorises a town. James Brolin looks serious, while the most memorable thing about his leading lady, Kathleen Lloyd, is her leather trousers. The basis of the car is unknown, but the custom job was the work of George Barris which makes the film worthy. It weighed three tons and had its front and rear wings raised 18 inches to look more menacing.

Christine
US, 1983, 110mins, colour
Dir: John Carpenter

From a Stephen King novel of the same name, this is the tale of a teenager who lovingly rebuilds a 1958 Plymouth Fury. That's fine until the car starts to become jealous of the lad's girlfriends and kills them.

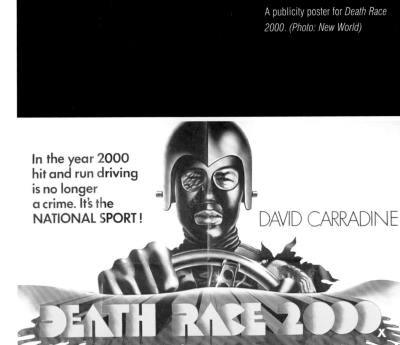

A publicity poster for *Death Race 2000*. (Photo: New World)

In the year 2000 hit and run driving is no longer a crime. It's the NATIONAL SPORT!

DAVID CARRADINE

DEATH RACE 2000

DAVID CARRADINE in 'DEATH RACE 2000', starring SIMONE GRIFFETH and SYLVESTER STALLONE Screenplay by ROBERT THOM and CHARLES B. GRIFFITH · Based on a story by IB MELCHIOR · Produced by ROGER CORMAN · Directed by PAUL BARTEL Released by **focus film distributors**

Another car with a mind of its own working up a sweat in the garage in the film *Christine*. (Photo: Columbia/ Delphi/Pictorial Press Limited)

Back to the Future
US, 1985, 116mins, col
Dir: Robert Zemeckis
The notorious Irish-built De Lorean sports car was still a symbol of all that was poorly conceived when the first – and much the best – of the *Back to the Future* films was released. It made an ironic time-machine in which to send Michael J. Fox back to the 1950s when he could change events and make a new future for his dysfunctional family.

Bad Taste
NZ, 1987, 90mins, colour
Dir: Peter Jackson
'Watch out aliens – here comes Derek!' Lord Crumb and his alien hordes invade New Zealand with the sole intention of turning its populace into hamburgers. But the Governor-General retaliates by dispatching Derek (Mr Jackson) and the boys. What chance does Lord Crumb have against a hero who drives a converted 105E Anglia Disabled Vehicle – complete with Sgt. Pepper silhouettes in the lower windscreen? Yes, the boys are tough – one drives a Morris Minor 1000 whilst another hardy soul barely complains at Crumb exploding his Capri 1600XL Mk1 – 'I should have bought a Volvo,' he merely grumbles. All this drama in a film made over a four-year period by Jackson plus friends and family for $NZ 250,000. Genuinely enjoyable unless the sight of sheep and early Ford Capris being exploded offends.

Crash
US, 1996, col, 96min
Dir David Cronenburg
Based on a novel by J.G Ballard *Crash* was a controversial film about a group of sexually malfunctioning individuals who could only achieve satisfaction by witnessing or being involved in car accidents. The film outraged *Daily Mail*-reading middle England and was the subject of much controversy but was eventually released uncut in the UK.

heroes & villains

the good, the mad and the ugly

A trip down a ravine leaves David
Niven and young passenger sooty
faced and the Triumph Herald
somewhat shattered in *Paper Tiger*.
*(Photo: Maclean and Co/Pictorial
Press Limited)*

THE RULES CONCERNING FILM archetypes are simple. Heroes never have to lock their car doors and always know where the controls are on an unfamiliar model. Villains are surrounded by acolytes and tend to favour whitewall tyres and louche paint finishes. So, here is a handy primer with which to while away even the most banal of screenplays.

In the late 1950s, the American social commentator Vance Packard noticed how 'educated' Americans, keen to display their 'individuality' and innate taste, tended to drive either very second-hand domestic models or new European imports such as Volkswagens. The few new American marques that might be chosen were from outside of the Big Three's province; Packards, Ramblers and even Checkers. Obviously, mainstream Hollywood films could use such theorising as a very convenient form of visual shorthand, not least in the too-little-seen William Goldman adaptation of *Harper* in which Paul Newman drives a Porsche 356. The car is the ideal choice for the character – a cultivated bachelor private eye of insouciant mien – whereas an E-type would have been too flamboyant and a new 911 slightly too ostentatious. Likewise, Clint Eastwood's tatty XK150 in *Play Misty for Me* is a totally appropriate choice for the character of a small town DJ whom Eastwood himself described as 'a typical big fish in a small pond'.

There are countless other examples of this phenomenon ranging from the subtle to the blindingly obvious. In *Joe versus The Volcano* Tom Hanks drives a 1957 Rambler American, so even a non-automotive audience can guess he is an 'individual' kind of a guy. Billy Crystal plays an English teacher in *Throw Momma from the Train*, so naturally he drives a Saab 96 V4, whereas Woodward and Bernstein travel to their meetings with *Deep Throat* in a Volvo Amazon. British cars are rarer in this category, but there is always Richard Dreyfuss's Land Rover in *Stand by Me* or Marsha Mason's Morris Minor Convertible in *Two Days in the Valley*. The BMW 2002 in *Silkwood* is particularly interesting; it displays the era prior to the marque's change of image in the 1980s when a 2002 might still be bracketed as 'quirky'.

But the first choice for any Hollywood individualist is the Citroën DS, from the Safari in *Clockers* to the Pallas in *The Rugrats Movie*.

A second group of individuals are the anti-heroes who have neither the funds nor the inclination to follow the latest automotive trends. Can any Robert Mitchum fan envisage *Thunder Road* with the latest in '58 Mercury Breezeways in place of the black '41 models? Inspector Harry Callaghan is a poor-but-honest cop with leather patches on his sports jacket, so Frank Bullitt's Mustang would be a wholly inappropriate choice of car. My own favourite is William Hartnell in *Hell Drivers*; he may be a transport manager who is on the take but that hasn't altered his taste for demob suits and 103A Series Ford Populars. Even more seldom seen are the upper class conservative individuals pitting themselves against a bureaucratic system – Bristol 406-driving Dirk Bogarde in *Victim* being one of a select few.

We have already encountered this dependable sort in the 'British Comedy' chapter, but it is always worth noting how our manly heroes show their devotion to tradition in their choice of car: old money = old cars, especially before the advent of the MoT test. Alternatively, when one considers how a British film hero might also drive the most mundane form of transport imaginable, then Jack Hawkins's use of a Vanguard Vignale in *The League of Gentlemen* (q.v.) makes perfect sense.

With regard to the younger leading men, one recalls PC Michael Caine flagging down Edward Judd's Series MM Minor in *The Day the Earth Caught Fire*. This use of unobtrusive cars lasted well into the era of anti-Bond films with Harry Palmer's MkIII Zodiac and the A55 Farina in *The Deadly Affair* being to the fore. Another use for a mundane vehicle is to anchor a lead character played by a major star – Sean Connery's north country CID Sergeant, in *The Offence*, wears a car coat and trilby, so his Morris 1100 should come as no surprise. By contrast, Rod Steiger, with Edinburgh accent and black Zephyr-Six MkIV in *Three into Two Won't Go* appears totally bizarre at every viewing.

To both British and French cinema after the Second World War, the American car was the embodiment of the menace of 'Coca Cola-Colonisation', driven by types who were at best suburban counter-jumpers and at worst criminals. Even more damningly, many of these so-called Yank tanks were either Canadian-built in the case of British films or Belgian-assembled for the French market. This demonisation of American machinery occurs across most genres – Peter Sellers's Oldsmobile in *Never Let Go*, or the Oldsmobile in *Mon Oncle*. Yet further down the scale from such vulgarity were the local interpretations of Americana ranging from Jean Gabin's Ford Vedette in *Touchez Pas au Grisbi* to the Vauxhall Victor Super in *A Taste of Honey*. As driven by Robert Stephens, playing a car dealer so inept that he cannot even run to a Cresta, the Victor is seen as but another aspect of ersatz Americana sweeping Macmillan-era England – with British rock and roll, neon-lit coffee bars and a car that, although resembling a squashed '56 Pontiac, at least boasted two-speed windscreen wipers.

Although the term 'rotter' isn't in common parlance in the USA, even a casual filmgoer cannot help noticing that if a Hollywood film doesn't boast an English villain it can always have a Harvard-educated American in a European car. By the 1980s the equivalent would be James Spader in a BMW 3-Series, but the inherent anti-Americanism of the character remains a constant factor. Laurence Harvey in *Butterfield 8* may or may not be American – he plays the part with a RADA accent at any rate – but his choice of cream Mercedes-Benz 300d saloon both displays his elitist nature and helps to mask the actor's total boredom with the part. However, Harvey's performance in the two 'Joe Lampton' films is far more rewarding, in addition to displaying the British attitude to European cars prior to the 1970s. Certainly the Maserati Quattroporte at the conclusion of *Life at the Top* would have been as far removed from the more expected Super-Snipe as would be *La Strada* from *Doctor in the House*, but even mundane European transport would have seemed almost as exotic to the 1960s British filmgoer. The Renault Carravelle in *The Pumpkin Eater* may

have been little more than a re-bodied R8 but it certainly was styled with brio, whilst the Mercedes-Benz 220 in *Georgy Girl* may have been not so far removed from a West German taxi-cab but at least it had a white steering wheel.

To Catch a Thief
US, 1955, 97mins, colour
Dir: Alfred Hitchcock

Apart from the lush Riviera scenery, some crisp dialogue and a charismatic star (Cary Grant) the main thing to recommend *To Catch a Thief* is the car chase with Grace Kelly (it was her last film before marrying Prince Rainier) at the wheel of a Sunbeam Talbot Alpine pursued by policemen in a Citroën Traction. It was nail-biting stuff in 1955 although now looks rather tame.

And God Created Woman
(aka Et Dieu... Créa la Femme)
Fr, 1956, 95mins, colour
Dir: Roger Vadim

Brigitte Bardot bares her bottom in the name of art as she is torn between John-Louis Trintignant, Christian Marquand and Curt Jurgens but since Curt drives a silver Lancia Aurelia B24 Spyder, he's surely in with more than a sporting chance. Both Lancia and *derrière* benefit hugely from the widescreen colour photography of St Tropez. A 1988 remake featured Rebecca De Mornay and her bottom but no Lancias, so best to give it a miss.

Mon Oncle
Fr, 1958, 110mins, colour
Dir: Jacques Tati

Amilcar-driving 6ft 5in eccentric M. Hulot (Tati) arrives at the sterile automated home of the Arpels, his sister and brother-in-law. To show how dreadfully nouveau riche the Arpels really are, Tati has them taking delivery of a Belgian-built Oldsmobile rather than the Roland Barthes-approved DS19. A charming view of a France where a car cigarette lighter was still novelty enough to be included in a gag routine.

The League of Gentlemen

GB, 1959, 116mins, b&w
Dir: Basil Dearden

The League of Gentlemen is concerned with Lt. Col. Jack Hawkins's attempts to lure seven ex-officers and gentlemen away from decadent civilian life and the effects of women (or young men in the case of Captain Stevens) and to give them a common goal; robbing a bank. In this enterprise, his 'adjutant' is the cad's cad Major Race (Nigel Patrick) who naturally drives an Alvis Grey Lady – certainly not a Jaguar for that would be straying into Terry-Thomas territory. Of course, for the campaign to work, sacrifices must be made, not least the Colonel exchanging his Rolls-Royce Phantom drophead for a Vanguard Vignale to double as an army staff car when raiding an army camp.

To reveal the end would be to ruin one of cinema's best heist films (forget *Ocean's Eleven*), but suffice to say that the scene with a Hillman Husky being driven up the tailboard of an Austin pantechnicon possibly influenced a certain Michael Caine film. *The League of Gentlemen* also provided the last great starring role for Jack Hawkins, an early one for Oliver Reed, and displayed a post-war England where AA patrolmen still saluted all members, gentlemen or not.

The Challenge

GB, 1960, 101mins, b&w
Dir: John Gilling

You'll find this one lost somewhere in the TV listings at 1am on a weekday morning, a nominal A-movie starring the never-to-be repeated line up of Jayne Mansfield, Anthony Quayle and Edward Judd (fans of 1970s road safety films should recognise Mr Judd's insistent tones – 'Imagine this swiss roll is a speeding Austin Maxi. Imagine this Cadbury's Chocolate Finger is a motorbike. Watch what happens!') Don't stay up for it but tape it for the car chase. The credits

Demonic Nuffield dealer Peter Sellers confronts honest Anglia-driving Richard Todd in *Never Let Go*. (Photo: Rank/Julian Wintle/Leslie Parkin/Pictorial Press Limited)

Alan Bates, Millicent Martin and her Alfa Spyder in *Nothing but the Best*. (Photo: Anglo-Amalgamated/Domino/Pictorial Press Limited)

A JULIAN WINTLE — LESLIE PARKYN PRODUCTION
RICHARD TODD   PETER SELLERS
ELIZABETH SELLARS   in
NEVER LET GO
with   (X)
ADAM FAITH   CAROL WHITE
RANK FILM DISTRIBUTORS LTD.

quickly establish the scenario: cut to a MkVII Jaguar parked by a deserted warehouse, at its wheel is a nearly unrecognisable Miss Mansfield in a brunette wig. A gang of trilby-hatted ne'er-do-wells pile into the MkVII and speed off, but, as is *de rigueur* for a film of this genre, a Wolseley 6/80 Traffic Car spots them and the pursuit begins, followed by cutaways to Mansfield spinning the Jaguar's four-spoked steering wheel, reverse shots of the black Wolseley with only its 'POLICE' sign and illuminated oval grille badge visible. Eventually, Jayne tightly corners the Jaguar past a concrete 'Keep Left' bollard but no Wolseley 6/80 is built for such treatment. The police car overturns, killing the driver. But the passenger, Detective-Sergeant Edward Judd survives and swears vengeance. Now go to bed.

Never Let Go
GB, 1960, 90mins, b&w
Dir: John Guillermin

A scrapyard in West London circa 1960. As a freight train rattles past a dismembered Citroën Light 15, Fred Griffiths passes John Bailey a bundle of notes. The soundtrack music is sparse and menacing, all insistent bongo drums and bass piano notes. Cut to mechanic Nigel Stock respraying a Minx. Cut to a Yank Tank pulling up outside 'The Victory Cafe', a sleazy haunt of teddy boys somewhere in Paddington. The driver, a spivvy looking man in his mid-forties, beckons over Adam Faith and hands him a piece of paper. Close-up of paper – a list of cars finishing with '1959 Ford Anglia'. Cue opening credits, accompanied by John Barry's big band jazz theme, filmed over a parked Ford Anglia 105E De Luxe . . .

This is the struggle of one little man (commercial traveller Richard Todd) to retrieve his Ford Anglia from a brutal Buick-driving thug played by Peter Sellers in one of his best ever performances. A short, rather desperate figure with a Croydon accent, Todd is treated with contempt by his clients, his sales director and (as we shall see) police inspectors and gang-bosses alike. The Anglia is his attempt to prove to his director, and himself, that he is

indeed with-it and a part of this brave new post-war world. Very rarely seen on British television, the black and white cinematography of *Never Let Go* captures some wonderful vignettes of pre-Swinging London, from the muscle-bound David Lodge fleeing justice (people fled differently in 1960) to the low angle shot of the police 6/90s skidding under a railway arch towards Nigel Stock's workshop (naturally one of the police drivers is Mr Wadham).

Victim
GB, 1961, 100mins, b&w
Dir: Basil Dearden

Although disguised as a murder mystery *Victim* was the first British film to deal seriously with homosexuality. Dirk Bogarde was a Bristol 406-driving barrister with a seemingly straight home life who was being blackmailed by a former boyfriend.

The Running Man
GB, 1963, 103mins, colour
Dir: Carol Reed

Laurence Harvey plays a light aircraft pilot who fakes his death for the insurance money, moves to Spain with his wife (Lee Remick) and buys a Lincoln Continental clap-door convertible. Things turn nasty when insurance investigator Alan Bates starts sniffing around in his Austin Cambridge. A chase ensues along mountain roads. Crap film, great Lincoln.

Nothing but the Best
GB, 1964, 99mins, colour
Dir: Clive Donner

Estate agent Jimmy Brewster (Alan Bates) is a Joe Lampton-like figure totally devoid of morals. In a film where old money effortlessly absorbs the new, all Jimmy has to do to achieve his E-type plus Alfa Romeo 1600 Spyder-driving girlfriend is to have his own parents shipped off to Australia as '£10 Pommies' and pay soused public school remittance man Denholm Elliott for the secrets of successful counter jumping. *Nothing but the Best* is still required viewing for all embryonic estate agents and property dealers.

Alfie

GB, 1966, 108mins, colour
Dir: Lewis Gilbert

The shadow of Alfie Elkins haunted Michael Caine's career until the end of the 1960s – Charlie Croker (*The Italian Job*) is Alfie in an Austin Cooper S and Pte. Tosh Hearne (*Too Late the Hero*) is Alfie in a Medical Corps uniform. The posters didn't help either – 'Michael Caine IS Alfie'. But the chief culprit has to be the future Sir Maurice Micklewhite himself, for giving such an immaculate character performance in only his second leading role.

Alfie was filmed in 1965 and released in 1966. Despite the fact that it is perceived as the epitome of a 'Swinging London Film', Alfie is portrayed as virtually a 1950s relic. The car he takes such pride in owning is a 1955 E-Series Velox and his wardrobe runs to double-breasted blazers with pseudo-regimental badges. In fact, much of Alfie is fake; the cars he drives belong to the firm he chauffeurs for – 'Nice isn't it,' he croons whilst polishing a black Series III Super-Snipe prior to taking a party of licensed victuallers on a beano to Brighton. Furthermore, Alfie isn't above using a Silver Cloud to seduce both the wife of one of his friends, leading to the infamous abortion sequence, and pick-up a mentally disturbed teenager at an A-road lorry drivers' pull in. 1965 Britain was still very much pre-motorway and very, very un-swinging. Incidentally, for some of the scenes the R-R was towed, Michael not actually holding a driving licence.

At the conclusion our anti-hero has only a wardrobe of Terylene and mohair suits and a 10-year-old Vauxhall. As we focus on Caine's cobra-like stare, he even confesses to a loss of peace of mind. It takes an actor of the highest calibre to engage any sympathy for such a figure, and not for nothing was Caine nominated for his first Oscar (as indeed was the theme song, subsequently massacred by Cilla Black but here sung by Cher). Gilbert's direction contains too many longueurs but does leave us with a London of seedy bedsits, Ford Thames Traders and red double-decker buses.

Harper
(aka The Moving Target)

US, 1966, 121mins, colour
Dir: Jack Smight

An attempt to re-invent the Chandleresque school in the '60s idiom with Paul Newman burbling around LA in a rather self-consciously beaten-up Porsche 356.

The Graduate

US, 1967, 105mins, colour
Dir: Mike Nichols

'Can you handle a European shift?' There is a myriad of books concerning the significance of *The Graduate* on both 1960s counter-culture and the development of Hollywood (Peter Biskind's *Easy Riders*, *Raging Bulls* being my own favourite), so we'll limit ourselves here to noting how well the Alfa suits Mr Hoffman. Had Mike Nichols cast Robert Redford as Benjamin Braddock, then a TR4A or perhaps a late-model Porsche 356C would have suited those waspish good looks. They certainly wouldn't have tallied with Hoffman's short stature and nervous persona. A Sprite or a Spitfire would have served only to emphasise his lack of height, and might well have rendered Benjamin immature as opposed to insecure, whereas the Alfa Romeo highlights the character's self-perceived status as an outsider in a land of swimming pools and immaculate lawns.

Yet for a rebel, Benjamin remains a bourgeois and, above all, thoroughly confused young man in Mike Nichols's take on 1967 middle-class America. There is no mention of the Vietnam war (or indeed Benjamin's possible conscription) in LA suburbia and our hero still dresses in a blue blazer to seduce Mrs Robinson. He is a rebel who still lives at home and, although affecting to despise his parents' lifestyle, Benjamin takes great delight in piloting his graduation present, the red Duetto Spyder.

But it is precisely this degree of honesty in Hoffman's performance and Nichols's direction that makes *The Graduate* date far better than many a 'Hollywood-hippy movie' and saves it from being merely an interesting period

Slightly tarnished Michael Caine
(Alfie) with Millicent Martin (Siddie)
and the Vauxhall Velox in *Alfie*.
(Photo: Paramount/BFI Collections)

Dustin Hoffman driving the red Alfa
Spyder in *The Graduate*.
*(Photo: UA/Embassy/Pictorial Press
Limited)*

Steve McQueen, Faye Dunaway and the Corvair-engined beach buggy in *The Thomas Crown Affair*.
(Photo: UA/Mirisch/Simkoe/Solar/ Pictorial Press Limited)

Edward Fox doing an alfresco respray on the Alfa Spyder that featured in *The Day of the Jackal*.
(Photo: Universal/Warner/Universal France/Pictorial Press Limited)

piece. *The Graduate* may have been virtually parodied to death, Alfa Romeo may have brought out a version of the Spyder called 'The Graduate' in the 1980s (when else?) but the imagery of Mr Hoffman accelerating a sports car made when the Alfa Romeo name really had a potent meaning still pervades. Even if he does eventually take up a career in plastics.

The Thomas Crown Affair
US, 1968, 102mins, colour
Dir: Norman Jewison

Showing McQueen at the height of his powers *The Thomas Crown Affair* is the story of a property tycoon who masterminds a bank robbery, just to spice life up a little, and is then pursued by a beautiful insurance investigator (Faye Dunaway) who proceeds to fall in love with him. Maybe it's his blue Mulliner Park Ward Silver Shadow two door Coupé that does it, although Miss Dunaway is hardly found lacking in the wheels department: she drives a Ferrari 275GTB Nart Spider, one of only nine ever built. The beach buggy scene is another memorable moment in a film that looks a bit too slick for its own good now.

Sudden Terror
(aka Eyewitness)
GB, 1970, 92mins, colour
Dir: John Hough

The original poster for this entry boasted 'The Most Exciting Car Chase Since *Bullitt*!' but a closer inspection reveals that one of the vehicles in the chase is a Herald saloon which, with all due deference to the Owners Club, is not quite on the same plane as a Mustang. Furthermore, the drama takes place in Malta where there isn't all that much space in which to stage a lengthy pursuit. Still, the plot of a teenage boy witnessing the assassination of an African Leader in a Mercedes-Benz 300 Convertible allows for some splendidly driven police Oxford Farinas plus the Peters Bowles and Vaughn as the baddies and David Lodge as an amazingly unauthentic Maltese policeman.

The Day of the Jackal
GB/France, 1973, 142mins, colour
Dir: Fred Zinnemann

The Day of the Jackal is the only really good film that has ever come out of one of Frederick Forsyth's novels. It tells with clinical detail the story of a plot to kill de Gaulle by the OAS in the early '60s using a professional assassin, played here by the excellent Edward Fox. Although there is no attempt, other than with the vehicles central to the story, to be faithful to the period in which the action is supposed to take place (there were no Renault 16s or Peugeot 504s in the early '60s yet we clearly see them driving around in the background) this doesn't seem to matter because Zinnemann's direction doesn't allow the mind to wander. This is a good story beautifully told. DS Citroëns in ministerial black feature heavily (naturally) but the main car interest comes from the Alfa Guilia Spyder driven by Fox and bought specially for the assignment. Fox hides his rifle in a special compartment in the exhaust and drives the car with great verve. When the Gendarmerie begin to close in he resprays the Alfa at the side of the road using some manner of hair dryer, but the Giulia meets an ignominious end when Fox falls asleep at the wheel and crashes into a Peugeot 403.

The Mackintosh Man
GB/USA, 1973, 98mins, colour
Dir: John Huston

A minor Huston film perhaps, but with the exception of *Escape to Victory* even a minor Huston film is eminently watchable, not least for the scene in which special agent Paul Newman escapes from the baddies' Mercedes-Benz 190 Fintail in a very early Ford Transit pick-up. As the Mercedes is at least eight years old it comes as no surprise when it is wrecked on the cliff-tops of Western Ireland but the chase is exciting enough to compensate for Mr Newman's really dire Australian accent in the opening reels.

The Mean Machine
US, 1974, 127mins, colour
Dir: Robert Aldrich

Burt Reynolds is a drunken burnt-out football star who steals his girlfriend's Citroën SM ('No, you're not taking my Mahserati ...') and takes on the local fuzz in an impressive chase at the beginning of the film. The car ends up in the docks and Reynolds in gaol where he is then blackmailed into knocking a prison football team into shape.

Paper Tiger
GB, 1974, 99mins, colour
Dir: Ken Annakin

David Niven atones for *Casino Royale* and *The Brain* with his best performance since *Separate Tables* as a retired schoolmaster with fantasies of a non-existent Second World War commission in the Commandos. Set in an un-named Commonwealth country in the Far East, the film is best remembered by motor enthusiasts for having Niven and chum emerge unscathed from a Herald 1200 convertible sans seatbelts that has just plunged down a ravine at approximately Warp Speed 10.

All the President's Men
US, 1976, 138mins, colour
Dir: Alan J. Pakula

This well-played reconstruction of the Watergate affair, with Robert Redford and Dustin Hoffman as the *Washington Post* reporters, is an early example of European cars being used to signify liberal characters in an American film: VW Beetles and Volvo Amazons in this case.

The Bitch
GB, 1979, 89mins, colour
Dir: Gerry O'Hara

What can be written about a film that believes Joan Collins, the Rank Charm School alumna with that wonderfully 1950s piping voice, to be the corseted embodiment of sexual allure? Quite possibly the same mentality that believes the Panther DeVille, one of the few luxury cars to be fitted with Austin 1800 doors, to be the epitome of urban chic.

Rough Cut
US, 1980, 112mins, colour
Dir: Don Siegel

Not one of Don Siegel's better moments, *Rough Cut* was the story of a retiring Scotland Yard Inspector (David Niven) who first confronts then joins a jewel thief (Burt Reynolds). To keep a low profile Reynolds's character tooled around London in a gold Rolls-Royce Corniche drophead with a nondescript registration mark.

time & place

a sense of period

AN EFFECTIVE WAY to anchor a historical production to its period and place is to use the relevant cars, and whilst many film-makers have grasped this to good effect – the *Godfather* series for instance – others have got it so wrong that even those with minimal interest in cars get distracted by the inappropriate vehicles sharing screen space with the actors. True car enthusiasts – and classic car enthusiasts in particular – have a solemn duty to perform when gauging a film's historical accuracy. They must utter the time-honoured cry of 'That car wasn't even a prototype in 19xx!' or, more succinctly, 'That's wrong!' despite the risk of disapproval from other cinemagoers or occupants of the living room.

The Ragman's Daughter is a nearly-forgotten 1972 adaptation of an Alan Sillitoe novel but it does contain an intriguing sequence in which our long-haired hero is dragged into a Mk2 Zephyr police car. This is at first confusing – surely even the most budget-conscious county constabulary wouldn't be running a patrol car aged 10-plus years – until the viewer realises that the narrative is set circa 1962. Here, a period car is essential to timing the plot – especially when the leading cast members continue to sport contemporary barnets. Another good example is Hammer's 1968 version of *The Devil Rides Out* – it may well boast the finest Lancias to been seen in British cinema but it also has Patrick Mower (no comment) as a juvenile lead with a Carnaby Street hairstyle – and then there's *Borsalino* with a breathtaking array of 1930s French cars and some actors with very luxuriant locks.

However, just as there are clubs and enthusiasts for the most tedious of cars, so there are films of such low ambition that it would be churlish to criticise them for period errors. *Escape to Athena* has Greek partisans introducing the Beatles haircut to occupied Greece and the spectacle of Roger Moore as a Nazi officer, so who would notice the premature appearance of the occasional Fiat 1100R?

Let's Get Laid has Mr Robin Askwith sporting a 1960s haircut and cycling along streets littered with 1950s vehicles, so obviously this is a 1970s film set in the Second World War, and any anachronistic period cars in *Porky's* or *Lemon Popsicle* are soon forgotten by the viewer when he/she is confronted with 33-year-old high school students. *National Lampoon's Animal House*, the film responsible for the hideous 'frat pack' genre, has a pretty decent grasp of period. The clothes and the hairstyles look authentic, the villainous preppie drives a criminally orange MGA and the main errors concern the 1964 Lincoln Continental and the 1963 Kingsmen version of *Louie Louie* on the soundtrack, for the setting is 1962 – so often the year that Hollywood uses to symbolise the 'end of innocence'.

Related to this group are films that boast an equally low budget but work hard to achieve a sense of time via the acting, script, direction and the *mise en scène*. *Withnail & I* and *Quadrophenia* are both individually listed in this book, but there are also films such as *The Wanderers*, which chart the changing face of youth culture circa1963 as tailfins subside and the Mustang lurks in the wings, or the British TV film *East of Ipswich* where suburban paterfamilias John Nettleton in his Mk1 A55 De-Luxe seethes in middle-class rage as he is overtaken by Alan Cuthbertson's Rover 100.

The duotone blue and cream Bedford CA Utilicom in *East is East* is equally well used, and although there are few cars in *Prick Up Your Ears* they are all adroitly deployed, none less than the police 6/110 that approaches the rather occupied gentlemen's convenience. Finally, there's a personal favourite, 1966's *Daleks – Invasion Earth 2150 AD* which valiantly attempts to convey a quasi-Second World War London atmosphere despite the fact that our heroes outrun the villainous pepper pots in a 1950 Morris Commercial. At least none of the protagonists seemed to notice that the Daleks had Morris Minor indicator lights in their heads. *Invasion Earth* belongs in the fantasy sub-genre, which allows all manner of experiments in art direction. The Coen Brothers' *Hudsucker Proxy*, set in the 1950s, boasts set design more akin to the 1930s, *The Borrowers* is set in a world where every human drives a Morris Minor, Oxford or Six (although they drive right-hand drive cars on the right à la pre-1967 Sweden) and Morrises make an appearance in Peter Jackson's *Meet The Feebles* and his 1950s-set suburban zombie comedy *Braindead*. *Mousehunt*, although ostensibly a contemporary late-1990s film, has Lee Evans driving a Volvo PV544 that complies perfectly with his decaying and soot-belching factory.

When the viewer sees names such as Coppola or Scorsese (for argument's sake) on a film's credits, they have the right to expect every detail to be as accurate as possible. The cars alone are reasons for watching the first two *Godfather* films (only fans of big Italian saloons should bother with *The Godfather III*) whilst *Goodfellas* has respectable Volvo 200 driving mobsters. It is when high-budget and over-hyped epics make error after crass error that the viewer must pick up his/her pen, and here are some choice examples – the 1965 Humber Hawk police car in the 1963-sequence in *Scandal*, many of the vehicles in the horrendous 'chirpy cockney' gangster biopic *Buster* (did the Met really use Wolseley 1500s?) and the 1950s Ford Vedette in the Second World War drama *Memphis Belle*.

The exception to this litany of inaccuracies is where the film is of such a standard that any glaring motoring errors are soon forgotten. Take the 1954 Danny Kaye vehicle in *Knock on Wood* for example – it may feature a London of left-hand-drive cars but it also boasts (if my memory is correct) the one-and-only Triumph TRX prototype. Typically, the director attempts to recreate the very recent past by foregrounding the period vehicles whilst paying scant attention to the background. Much of 1962's *The Manchurian Candidate* is actually set in the 1950s, although the streets of Washington DC seem to have rather a lot of Falcons and Valiants. 1968's *The Boston Strangler* is again set in the recent past – the early 1960s – and although the black-and-white police cars are authentic Ford Galaxie 500s, the background extras are frequently mini-skirted, and although both Alfa Romeo and Citroën DS fans find *The Day of The Jackal* (see 'cops & robbers') essential viewing, even they could not fail to notice the Simca 1501s, Renault 12s and Peugeot 304s in 1963 Paris. This technique was employed in the adaptation of Graham Swift's *Last Orders* where the late 1980s sequences had Ray Winstone's Mercedes-Benz S-Class foregrounded against a background of Mondeos and Vectras (although a Wedge Princess and a Marina appear from time to time) but, as with the other films in the group, such anachronisms really do not detract from the narrative's power – not a claim that any film under the next sub-heading could make.

Here, the past isn't merely a foreign country but a nirvana of drive-ins, 'Mom & Pop' grocery stores and Chevrolet Bel Airs (Hollywood), or steam trains, Brylcreem, decency and side-valve Morris Minors (British cinema). Any foreground vehicle featured therein will sport immaculate coachwork and date from the year of the film's setting whilst background vehicles will be at least two years too young (you can almost hear the art director's standard two excuses – 'They look period,' or 'Old cars are just old cars').

Another challenge to a film-maker is not merely finding authentic vehicles but ensuring that they are appropriate to the central characters. *Spotswood*, an Australian comedy set in the late 1960s has Anthony Hopkins's repressed time and motion expert driving a Rover P6, but surely such an insular conservative chap would have favoured a Wolseley 24/80 or an Austin Freeway Six. I could also mention that some of the cars in *Absolute Beginners* don't look terribly accurate but that would be carping for carping's sake.

Why criticise at all? Well, largely because at the time of writing, the current cry of the historically illiterate is 'It happened before I was born', and it is very sad that people ignore the fascination of recreating the past properly. Just consider the MkX Jaguars in *Gangster No. 1*, the heroine of *Peggy Sue Got Married* in hysterics at her father's new Edsel (the year is 1960 so he really should have known better), the Vanguard estate car in *Dance with a Stranger* or *Coup de Foudre* (aka *Entre Nous*), where Michel Korski's pride in his new Renault Fregate symbolises his new bourgeois status. The past is too important to be ignored – otherwise we'll have more and more Austin FX4 taxis appearing in Second World War London.

Bonnie and Clyde

US, 1967, 111mins, colour
Dir: Arthur Penn

The famous demise of the couple in a machine-gunned
Ford V8 is all the more effective because of the use of cars
throughout the film – part of a flawless recreation of the
Depression era. 'They're young! They're in love! And they
kill people!' With this slogan the film's publicists promoted
Faye Dunaway and Warren Beatty in the title roles.

Because the fateful duo need their getaway vehicle to
work they get C. W. Moss to join their gang when he fixes
their car at a gas-station – 'dirt in the fuel line'. When he
identifies the car as a Ford, Bonnie corrects him – 'No, this
is a stolen Ford …'

Acting as getaway driver on the next job, CW carefully
reverse-parks the car outside the bank, only to find when
the guns are blazing that the space is too snug to get out
of. It's downhill from there. The real Bonnie and Clyde were
so impressed with the performance and reliability of their
beloved Ford V8 that they wrote a letter to Mr Ford in praise
of the car.

American Graffiti

US, 1973, 110mins, colour
Dir: George Lucas

This 1932 Ford Model A five-window coupé street rod, with
(probably) a Chevrolet V8 crammed into the engine bay
helped Lucas make this film's success a springboard for
the *Star Wars* project. Other cars included 1949 Mercury
lead-sled, a '58 Impala, the inevitable '55 Chevy and 'baby'
Thunderbird with a porthole hardtop driven by the film's
enigmatic female interest. A parade of non-modified
American '60s cars in mint condition helped generate a
highly commercial glow of nostalgia for a mythical America
of pre-Vietnam, pre-Watergate innocence. The action takes
place on a night in the life of a group of high school
graduates, teenagers unsure of what life holds in store for
them. To avoid the issue they spend their time indulging in
California's highly developed automotive culture, with its

A dance routine with John Travolta and others set on and around the mock-up hot rod in *Grease*. (Photo: Paramount/Pictorial Press Limited)

Sting on the Brighton front with other scooter-riding Mods in *Quadrophenia*. (Photo: Brent Walker/Pictorial Press Limited)

drive-ins and impromptu high street drag racing. British teenagers would have been lucky to own a clapped-out Austin Seven in 1962 yet here their North American contemporaries had access to all manner of exotic and dangerously high-powered machinery.

Cult DJ Wolfman Jack provides an authentic sound track to a film that gets the period detail absolutely right and catapulted its stars Richard Dreyfuss and Ron Howard into solidly successful careers, the latter in the TV series *Happy Days* (undoubtedly inspired by *American Graffiti*), although Harrison Ford would have to wait until *Star Wars* before his career found its feet again. *American Graffiti* cost $750,000 to make and grossed $55 million. It inspired many inferior imitators and spawned a trite sequel – set two years later in 1964 – *More American Graffiti*.

American Graffiti inspired a whole generation of wannabe British customisers and psuedo drag-racers, but somehow a rainy night in Guildford doesn't have quite the same romance.

Mr Ford, now 60, appears in TV adverts promoting Lancias in Europe.

Grease
US, 1978, 110mins, colour
Dir: Randall Kleiser

There were no hot-rods like this red mid-'40s Plymouth-based concoction in America in the 1950s, and garages certainly weren't full of pouting young men who looked delicious in overalls. But the film's stylised '50s nostalgia is cheerful enough to earn forgiveness and it successfully consolidated John Travolta's heart-throb star status after his initial success with *Saturday Night Fever*. There's a race between a '49 Mercury and an early-50s model in a storm drain, and Travolta sings a song about heads, four-on-the-floor and something called a 'dual quad lifter'.

The next time we saw Mr Travolta driving anything remotely cool was almost 20 years later in Quentin Attention's *Pulp Fiction* where, as a hitman with a sense of humour, he favours a Chevy Malibu.

Quadrophenia
GB, 1979, 120mins, colour
Dir: Franc Roddam

Imagine that you have been tasked with producing a film set some 15 years in the past and, just to make it more interesting, you have a minuscule budget. Aside from the problem that recapturing the recent past is a challenge, the narrative takes place in urban locales – so the easy option of a rural setting with far less anachronistic vehicles and road signs is denied to you. So, what's the solution?

Quadrophenia contains so many anachronisms in its early '60s setting that to list them all would fill both this book and its equally good-value sequel. There's the cinema poster for *Star Wars*, a dearth of oblong road signs, the Intercity 125 at a time when BR still used steam engines, the Morris 1100 on the scrapheap (the ADO16 did corrode badly, but after only three years?) and the streets seemed to be packed with Mk1 Vauxhall Cavaliers and MkIV Cortinas. Even some of the 'period' props are not entirely accurate: the Brighton police do arrive in authentic looking Oxford Farina Travellers but half of the uniformed extras sport long hair, the rockers look more Motorhead than Gene Vincent and there were no Jaguar 420s in 1965. Small wonder that some younger viewers become very confused as to the narrative's setting.

Now that this carping is dealt with, we can say that *Quadrophenia* is one of the best depictions of British youth since *Billy Liar*. The background details may be appalling but the actual plot, carried by its blend of the young (Phil Daniels, Leslie Ash, Toyah Willcox, Ray Winstone), the seasoned (Michael Elphick) and the frankly criminal (the late John Bindon) really does capture the problems of a young man who actually would spend a month's wages on a tailored silk Mod suit. Indeed, for one wonderful moment, when Daniels is carrying Miss Ash on his pillion, our hero really believes himself to be Tolen from *The Knack… and How To Get It*. Small wonder that Daniels is rather upset when a Morris LD GPO van crashes into his Vespa – 'You've killed my fucking scooter, Mr Postie Man!' he ad-libs to a genuinely shocked stunt driver.

Withnail & I
GB, 1986, 107mins, colour
Dir: Bruce Robinson

For any readers who might be scared off *Withnail & I* by the dread term 'cult', please don't be. *Withnail* is one of Britain's finest rites-of-passage movies, concerning itself with two out-of-work actors, Marwood and Withnail, escaping Camden Town and the fag end of Swinging London for a short holiday in a Lake District cottage belonging to Withnail's Uncle Monty. To reach Cumbria they use Withnail's powder blue Mk2 Jaguar, a car that is in such dire condition that it would barely make the banger circuit.

As Grant drunkenly steers the Mk2 through north London, you can almost smell the rotting leather upholstery and the mildewed carpet, but even though the Jaguar is missing various chromium trim, lamps and the offside wiper (i.e. the rather vital one) it retains the same faded dignity as its master. Yet, if one is going to be truly nitpicking, it is not quite the correct car for Mr Withnail. Leaving aside the Mk2's condition – even if it was a 1959 model, could it have deteriorated so fast over the next decade? – isn't a Jaguar a slightly parvenu choice for Withnail? Richard E. Grant's performance does somewhat resemble a gone-to-seed actor-luvvie of the Laurence Harvey school – it's as if Withnail was born 10 years too late – so maybe a down-at-heel Alvis Grey Lady or Riley RMB.

However, this is the only quibble in a film that tries so valiantly to recreate the then-recent past of 1969. The M1 sequences were clearly shot in one day – we see the same Bedford pantechnicon, A60 Farina, E-Series Wyvern and MkIII Zodiac on both journeys – but at least the motorway wasn't crammed with the G-plate Hunters and Victors a lesser film would have featured.

Monty's R-R Silver Wraith De Ville is the perfect transport for one who would have considered a Silver Cloud a little bit nouveau, let alone a Silver Shadow, and the P4 Rovers in the Lake District help to assist Robinson's depiction of a rural England that has barely made it to 1960, right down to the A/B button telephones. This is truly a wondrous *fin-de-siecle* picture, complete with Anthony Wise as 'Policeman 2' in the Morris J4 giving his memorable tribute to Lionel Jeffries in *The Two-Way Stretch*.

Tin Men
US, 1987, 112mins, colour
Dir: Barry Levinson

Danny DeVito and Richard Dreyfuss argue over Barbara Hershey, sales methods and how to buy the latest Cadillac in early '60s Baltimore. The two men's lives are changing, and so are the times. In the end, Dreyfuss doesn't care about the damage to his two-door hardtop Series Sixty-Two: he's a salesman who's seen the future – and it's in the unmistakable and far more durable shape of a VW Beetle.

Driving Miss Daisy
US, 1989, 99mins, colour
Dir: Bruce Beresford

The car is a Hudson Hornet. When Jessica Tandy sells it and Morgan Freeman buys it from the dealer, she's touched at the sentimental loyalty of her old retainer. Wrongly, it transpires: Freeman explains that he's made an astute investment in a solid car – and for once it's really true that the thing has had one lady owner.

Havana
US, 1990, 145mins, colour
Dir: Sydney Pollack

The Cadillac Eldorado convertible is an accurate 1955 model, helping transport Robert Redford back in time. The pity is that no-one could persuade him to alter his very post-sixties fringe. This year of 'Eldo', representing (as far as Americans are concerned) a more innocent era in US history, certainly features in more period drama about the 1950s and 1960s than it did in films that were contemporary to it. In the real Havana, cars like the Cadillac are still a common sight because of the American trade embargo imposed on Cuba since the 1950s. Director Pollack is probably best known for old-style films and, of course, *Tootsie*.

Below: Danny DeVito smashing the windows of Richard Dreyfuss's Cadillac Series Sixty-Two in *Tin Men*. *(Photo: Touchstone/Pictorial Press Limited)*

Bottom left: Jessica Tandy and Morgan Freeman in front of the Hudson Hornet in *Driving Miss Daisy*. *(Photo: Warner/Pictorial Press Limited)*

Bottom right: Robert Redford and Leno Olin with the Cadillac Eldorado behind in *Havana*. The Cadillac is virtually the sole evidence of the film's period setting. *(Photo: UIP/Universal/Pictorial Press Limited)*

The Lincoln Continental, with Warren Beatty, in the studio lot for *Bugsy*. (Photo: Columbia/Tri-Star/Pictorial Press Limited)

Opposite top: Miranda Richardson (Viv) at the wheel and Willem Dafoe (Tom) in the passenger seat of the Crossley in *Tom & Viv*. (Photo: Entertainment/Samuelson/Harvey Kass/IRS/British Screen/Pictorial Press Limited)

Anthony Hopkins and the paint-spattered Rover P6 in *Spotswood*. (Photo: Feature/Meridian/Smiley/Pictorial Press Limited)

Opposite bottom: A group photo of the Carmichael family in front of their Citroën DS Safari in *Crooklyn*. (Photo: Electric Triangle/Forty Acres & A Mule/Childhoods/Pictorial Press Limited)

Bugsy
US, 1991, 135mins, colour
Dir: Barry Levinson
The Lincoln Continental V12 driven by Warren Beatty in this film ended up in Manchester. Beatty played Benjamin 'Bugsy' Siegel, the gangster who transformed a little desert town called Las Vegas into a gambler's paradise.

Spotswood
Aus, 1991, 95mins, colour
Dir: Mark Joffe
The film is set in the late '60s, and the Rover P6 is a quintessential '60s design whose forward thrust and discreet tail fins knocked years off Auntie Rover's image. But even in Australia, where this film was made (and where you can still find plenty of unrusted P6s), the plastic chip-cutter grille replaced the elegant stainless steel of the original only in 1971. Anthony Hopkins stars as a time and motion expert investigating a shoe factory.

Tom & Viv
US/GB, 1994, 125mins, colour
Dir: Brian Gilbert
Whether Vivienne Eliot ever drove is not known. Certainly, her husband T. S. Eliot spent some of the prize money he won for *The Waste Land* on an Austin, though he continued to be driven around by Bertrand Russell in what he later described as 'a Morris Minor with no brakes'. Only car scholars would recognise the vintage Crossley, a Manchester-built tourer of the mid-to-late '20s, in the picture.

Crooklyn
US, 1994, 114mins, colour
Dir: Spike Lee
An out-of-work jazz musician struggling to bring up his family in '70s Harlem drives not the usual Ford Country Squire estate but a very out-of-place Citroën DS Safari. As if he didn't have enough problems.

chapter seven
motor racing
drama on and off the track

GENERALLY SPEAKING, there are two schools of motor racing film viewers – the *Le Mans* school and the *Grand Prix* supporters. The former will sit avidly through all two hours of Steve McQueen's pet project, with the understated (or distinctly muted) approach to acting and the very economical dialogue being mere distractions from the film's *raison d'être* – the cars. For a *Le Mans* fan, the excitement begins in the paddock as he (and it usually is a 'he') mentally notes all of the vehicles commonly seen in Europe at the turn of the 1970s and waits eagerly for his favourite teams to appear. By the time of the actual racing footage he will have nearly passed away with excitement.

Naturally, the *Le Mans* fan will also watch other films with a motor racing theme, but again only for the actual cars and the footage of the world's race tracks. The general strangeness of *Bobby Deerfield* will be overlooked in favour of the shots of Italian circuits, while the terminal dreadfulness of *The Betsy* will likewise be ignored – but this is not to infer that our viewer will limit himself to colour 'A' movies. Mr *Le Mans* will derive as many thrills from watching John Ireland in Roger Corman's *The Fast and The Furious* – and from identifying the stock footage that exemplifies many a Corman production – as he does from evaluating *Greased Lightning* for period anachronisms. He will scour the late-night TV schedules for re-runs of Exclusive Films' 1954 epic *Mask of Dust* featuring American import Richard Conte amidst genuine footage of Goodwood, and he might even watch Will Hay's *Ask a Policeman* if only to catch the Brooklands footage before the closing credits.

By contrast, a *Grand Prix* supporter loves the most banal aspects of your average motor racing epic – the romantic Man of Danger plots. Such films have all clichés present and correct from the granite-jawed driver himself (who generally spends more time posturing in a workshop than actually driving) to the tireless mechanic/engineer and the best chum (who generally has bought it by the fourth reel), and, of course, the ladies. Motor racing films are a sexist collection, by and large, usually requiring the female gender to look pretty in the paddock, make sandwiches, iron the hero's flannels and blub decoratively. *Grand Prix* has all of this, plus 'international' locations (as befitting a mid-1960s big-budget film) and an 'international' (and often over-dubbed) cast, as well as the benefits of cameos from genuine F1 drivers, with good old Graham Hill hamming it up with Equity's finest.

Of course, *Grand Prix* fans are also car enthusiasts, but if their twin passions for cars and melodrama can be combined then so much the better. To such chaps (and chaps they usually are), the guest appearance of a Fairthorpe Atom in *Checkpoint* is of equal importance to Anthony Steel's manly smile, and the actual circuit footage in *The Racers* has equal status with Gilbert Roland's splendid moustache and Kirk Douglas's clench-jawed intensity (could he have played the part any other way?). In fact our *Grand Prix* fan is probably a secret collector of Douglas Sirk melodramas and really believes that a racing epic must be shot in the finest Technicolor. It is the only true medium to highlight Bill Travers's steely determination and Sid James's unique Johannesburg-Cockney-Australian accent in *The Green Helmet* or the very low budget of *The Checkered Flag*. Only the glossiest of colour cinematography can capture the delights of *Red Line 7000* – the pain and the anguish of James Caan's macho hero (it is a Howard Hawks film after all) plus the twin advantages of an alleged cameo from Jerry Lewis and a very rare appearance of a MG 1100 Sports Sedan. Some cruel critics gave the last-mentioned the acting honours.

So, two differing approaches to motor racing dramas, and it is no coincidence that most of the films in this chapter are 'period' – the failure of certain Tom Cruise and Sylvester Stallone vehicles points to a current lack of interest. Meanwhile, the *Grand Prix* fan and the *Le Mans* supporter have plenty of opportunities to compare these sub-genres as they probably share a flat – their respective spouses left them years ago.

Johnny Dark

US, 1954, 85mins, colour

Dir: George Sherman

Tony Curtis designs, builds and races his own fuel-injected sports car in this action melodrama that was written with him in mind.

Good racing footage but sadly Tony doesn't get to say 'Yonda lies the castle of my Fadda'.

The Racers

US, 1955, 112mins, colour

Dir: Henry Hathaway

Despite a very promising cast that includes Kirk Douglas, Lee J. Cobb and Cesar Romero, you'll lose the will to live early on in this story of a Grand Prix driver in Europe. But there is some good footage and Kirk Douglas drives an HWM.

Checkpoint

GB 1956, 84mins, colour

Dir: Ralph Thomas

In terms of authenticity *Checkpoint* was a winner. It featured two genuine V12 Lagonda sports racing cars loaned personally by Aston Martin boss David Brown (a friend of director Ralph Thomas), not to mention the driving talents of Roy Salvadori and Reg Parnell. John Wyer, Aston's racing supremo, went out to Florence to help orchestrate the set-piece Le Mans start.

The film was an industrial espionage thriller based around a Mille Miglia-type event called the Arno-Alpini. The Lagondas are Warren Ingram cars for the purposes of the plot, and they are being beaten soundly in competition by the Italian Ermini team who have developed a radical device for increasing power. Warren Ingram (James Robertson-Justice) decides he must have the device for his cars and sends Stanley Baker to steal it.

Unfortunately Baker gets caught and has to shoot his way out of trouble, leaving a burning factory and a dead policeman in his wake. So Baker has to be smuggled out of

Stanley Baker gives his opinion of
Anthony Steel's acting in *Checkpoint*.
(Photo: Rank/BFI Collections)

Top: Sid James and Bill Travers (plus Roland Curram and Peter Collingwood) in the garage with the Lister Jaguar in *The Green Helmet*. *(Photo: MGM/Dr Steve Chibnall Collection)*

Bottom: Susan Hayward wandering along the trackside in *Stolen Hours*. *(Photo: UA/Mirisch/Pictorial Press Limited)*

A Team Lotus car with a 105E Anglia in the background in *The Young Racers*. *(Photo: Roger Corman/Author's collection)*

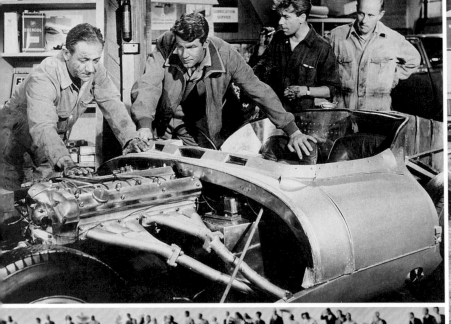

Italy, and the best way to do it is by pretending to be a co-driver in the Arno Alpini with Anthony Steel. Steel is suspicious but plays along until, just as they are approaching the finish and a certain win, Baker tells his driver to forget the race and head for Switzerland. There is a struggle and the car goes off the road, teetering above a lake on the edge of a cliff. Baker ends up in the lake, as does the Warren Ingram Lagonda – but don't worry it's just a glass fibre replica.

Checkpoint is worth watching for the racing footage. The crew went to Italy and covered the 1956 Mille Miglia with six cameras, cutting the footage into the film along with some film shot at that year's *Daily Express* Silverstone meeting. The Fairthorpe factory, located close to Pinewood in Buckinghamshire, doubles as the Ermini plant: the cars in the background when Baker is creeping about the factory are Fairthorpe Atoms!

The Green Helmet

GB, 1961, 88mins, b&w
Dir: Michael Forlong

Sid James, in his last straight role, plays (Australian!) mechanic and sidekick to Bill Travers, helping rebuild a Lister Jaguar and Travers's shattered nerves. The prototype steel-bodied Gordon Keble ('The Growler') provides serious eye-candy for the auto enthusiast. Very routine racing drama from a story by Australian author Jon Cleary who also wrote *Checkpoint*. There's another Aussie connection: look out for Jack Brabham.

Stolen Hours

GB, 1963, 97mins, colour
Dir: Daniel Petrie

A remake of the Bette Davis film *Dark Victory* set against a car racing background, this is the story of a dying millionairess who falls in love with her surgeon. Susan Hayward headlines beside square-jawed B-flicker stalwarts Michael Craig (the Captain in BBC's 'Triangle') and Edward (Think once, think twice, think bike) Judd.

The Young Racers

US, 1963, 84mins, colour
Dir: Roger Corman

Produced and directed by Roger Corman, better known for his work in the horror genre as well as mentor for young industry talent (Francis Ford Coppola was the sound man on this one) *The Young Racers* was shot in Europe and, as well as Mark Damon, William Campbell and Patrick Magee, featured real racing stars – including Bruce McLaren and Jim Clark – and real racing cars, including the then current Lotus contender. Filming at Aintree, Spa, Rouen and Monaco adds to the international flavour.

The Killers

US, 1964, 95mins, colour
Dir: Don Siegel

The Killers features some good early-'60s American racing footage and plenty of period American and European cars. It was directed by Don Siegel who later did *Dirty Harry*. Johnny North – John Cassavetes – races an AC Cobra, but things go wrong when he gets mixed up with duplicitous femme fatale Angie Dickinson, girlfriend of hoodlum Ronald Reagan. This was the last film he ever made.

Lee Marvin and Clu Gulager have been hired to shoot unprotesting Johnny but somewhere along the way they smell money and decide to investigate. They 'interview' Johnny's former mechanic in his workshop where several exotic European cars, including a Facel Vega HK500, are awaiting work. The plot involves a mailtruck heist: Angie Dickinson brings Cassavetes into Reagan's gang to do the driving using a 1959 Ford Fairlane mock police car. Johnny has to beef-up the suspension so the wallowing Ford sedan can keep pace with the truck. It all ends in tears of course and nobody of any significance is left standing.

Another version of *The Killers* – based on a story by Ernest Hemingway – was made in 1946 with Burt Lancaster and Ava Gardner. This 1964 version was originally made for television, but because of its violence was released in cinemas instead.

Red Line 7000

US, 1965, 110mins, colour
Dir: Howard Hawks

An early role for James Caan and a late, minor addition to
the canon of the great Hawks. Caan's best automotive
scene was yet to come – his death in *The Godfather* – but
this American stock-car drama has one great British feature:
the appearance of an MG 1100 among herds of macho
yanks.

Grand Prix

US, 1966, 179mins, colour
Dir: John Frankenheimer

Grand Prix is possibly the best film ever made about motor
racing. For six months in 1966, director John Frankenheimer
and his crew filmed Formula 1 races in the aftermath of the
real events, blending driving sequences with genuine race
footage shot at Monza, Spa-Francorchamps, Brands Hatch,
Zandvoort and Monaco. Streets in Monte Carlo were
specially closed for filming. The plot called for a French GP
but there wasn't one that season so Frankenheimer staged

a fake event at Clermont-Ferrand. As a piece of drama
Grand Prix is pretty ordinary. Between beautifully crafted
driving sequences – with a lot of groovy split-screen
treatments that become annoying after a while – the story of
American driver Pete Aron (James Garner) unfolds.

After being sacked from the Jordan BRM team (he is
blamed for an accident that puts his British team-mate Scott
Stoddard in hospital) he works briefly as a TV commentator,
then joins the Japanese Yamura team and ends up winning
the World Championship. It's the authentic pit lane scenes
of the period that get racing fans excited about Grand Prix,
and the shots inside racing teams' headquarters: the
Cooper Cars works in Byfleet, Surrey, doubles as the
Yamura factory.

While he isn't driving, Aron woos the estranged wife of
Stoddard. Yves Montand plays the ageing French heart-
throb Jean-Pierre Sarti, while the arrogant up-and-coming
Italian hothead Nino Barlini is played by Antonio Sabato,
who couldn't even drive.

Among the real drivers working as doubles on the film
was Phil Hill, who was allowed to film the start on the grid of

James Garner did his own driving in *Grand Prix*. Whatever happened to Brian Bedford (right)? *(Photo: MGM/ Pictorial Press Limited)*

Both real and dramatised motor racing is well used in *Un Homme et Une Femme*. (Photo: Les Films 13/Pictorial Press Limited)

Paul Newman taking the applause for another win in a Lotus Ford in *Winning*. (Photo: Universal/Newman-Pereman/Pictorial Press Limited)

UNIVERSAL PRESENTS

PAUL NEWMAN · JOANNE WOODWARD · ROBERT WAGNER

in "WINNING" A

TECHNICOLOR R   PANAVISION R

Music by DAVE GRUSIN   Written by HOWARD RODMAN

Directed by JAMES GOLDSTONE

Produced by JOHN FOREMAN

A JENNINGS LANG PRODUCTION

A UNIVERSAL/NEWMAN-FOREMAN PICTURE

the Belgian GP using a McLaren fitted with an Indycar engine. Sudden rain caused seven cars to crash. Other cameo roles were played by Graham Hill (Bob Turner), hamming enthusiastically, Richie Ginther (John Hearth) and Bruce McLaren (Douglas McClendon): even Paul Frère, the famous motoring journalist, puts in an appearance as himself. Chris Amon and Jochen Rindt were employed either to double for the actors or drive the GT40 camera car with the back and front taken off and one of the single seaters hitched to the back. The cars were Formula Juniors mocked-up by Jim Russell: MGM paid him new-for-old money to get the cars for filming.

James Garner was the only actor who did any serious driving, touching 140mph at one point on the rough banking at Monza. 'I was young and brave then. I'm not so brave any more …' he told Russell Bulgin in *Evo* magazine. 'The picture hired Bob Bondurant as a tech advisor to teach me how to drive. Because you really needed someone in that film who could drive. Yves Montand couldn't, Brian Bedford had just gotten his driver's licence. He went to the Jim Russell School and after a few days he said, "I can't do this; either double me or replace me."'

The fastest Brian Bedford ever went was 45mph. 'He was doubled by every racing driver we had,' said Garner. 'Antonio Sabato scared himself at Monte Carlo when he spun it in the pits in the first week. Montand would not take it out of third gear, so they put a governor on it and you could hear it go pop-pop-pop! everywhere. So I was the only one driving the cars, to my capabilities at least, but it sold the film by doing that.' Garner says that this was the movie he most enjoyed making. 'I must say the drivers were so kind to me. I made friends with them. Jochen Rindt was just a wonderful guy – and Richie Ginther.'

Acting worried the drivers as much as it worried Garner to be driving. 'It bothered them to be acting with actors. Graham came right out: nothing bothered him. He was such an outgoing personality anyway.'

After *Grand Prix*, Garner ran a race team for three years in sports car events and Formula A.

Un Homme et Une Femme
Fr, 1966, 102mins, b&w and colour
Dir: Claude Lelouch

Oscar winning story of a love affair between a French racing driver (Jean-Louis Trintignant) and a script girl (Anouk Aimée). Both have recently lost their partners, Anouk in a racing accident at Le Mans as we see in a flashback sequence. Slick looking with lots of motor racing – both real and dramatised – as a backdrop to the affair. Car interest includes rallying a Ford Mustang notchback in the Monte Carlo – and driving back through the night to Paris to declare his love for Anouk, test-driving of a GT40 at Montlhéry, and a Mustang convertible for social, domestic and pleasure use. The French always had a dubious penchant for supposedly stylish American machinery. Cars are afforded the rare dignity of being mentioned by name in the script, but the final reunion is, of course, set on a misty railway platform à la *Brief Encounter*.

Winning
US, 1969, 123mins, colour
Dir: James Goldstone

After doing all his own driving during filming, Paul Newman would develop a lifelong passion for racing. It tells the story of a successful racing driver whose marriage to Elora (Joanne Woodward) takes second place to his career, especially when his main rival Luther Erding (Robert Wagner) begins to out-drive him on a regular basis. In fact, he becomes so distracted that he doesn't notice Wagner wooing his wife until it's too late. He catches them at it in a motel room and simply walks out without a word. Like most motor racing films, *Winning* only comes to life when the cars are on the screen. Spectacular footage from Elkhart Lake, Wisconsin and Indianapolis is used, including a 17-car pile-up. Cameo appearances are made by racers Bobby Unsur and Tony Human. Ford obviously had a deal going as all the road cars featured wear the blue oval (Newman inspects the track in a dramatic '69 Thunderbird coupé with Landau bars) while the Indy cars are Lotus chassis with Ford power.

The unmistakable blue eyes of Steve McQueen in the hugely indulgent *Le Mans* which featured some amazing cars and a lot of bad acting. *(Photo: Solar/Cinema Center/Pictorial Press Limited)*

Le Mans

1971, US, 108mins, colour
Dir: Lee H. Katzin

If you don't enjoy cars or motor racing then *Le Mans* is a
punishing two hours. McQueen, in one of his most surly and
cardboard performances, plays second fiddle to the
machinery in a film that looks visually wonderful but never
allows you to get to know any of the characters. *Le Mans*
was a long-term pet project for McQueen but he was so
busy getting the car detail right he forgot to do any acting.
He doesn't speak for the first 40 minutes and thereafter
comes across as scowling. Even his friend Stirling Moss
called *Le Mans* 'piss poor', while McQueen's biographer
Christopher Sandford said: 'There's something wrong with
any picture where Jacky Ickx gives the best performance.'
You'll see other real drivers, like Derek Bell, David Piper (who
suffered a horrendous accident during the making of the
film) and Mike Hailwood. The film is at its best when the
various sports racing cars are on the screen, especially
when there is a shunt or two in the offing, or the viewer is put
in the cockpit in a point-of-view shot: there is a particularly
effective crash sequence using this technique with a fake
instrument shot to show us how quickly the action is
unfolding. But not even this, and excellent editing of the
450,000ft of film that was shot on this cocaine-fuelled piece
of self-indulgence, can save the gossamer-thin story line.

Bobby Deerfield

US, 1977, 123mins, colour
Dir: Sydney Pollack

Cars and the glamorous world of F1 racing are an incidental
backdrop to this tedious vehicle for Al Pacino who plays the
title character, a depressed driver who is arrogant about his
abilities and, just to complicate matters, falls in love with a
woman with an incurable illness.

Days of Thunder

US, 1990, 107mins, colour
Dir: Tony Scott

A 'vehicle' for Tom Cruise in every sense. Lots of noisy
American stock cars which, when they are not going round
and round, are crashing as only American stock cars can.
Actually, the filmed racing action is quite spectacular – in-
car cameras give a real feel for the speed – and goes some
way towards making up for the totally incredulous plot
about a driver (Cruise) who first time out in a stock car is
quick enough to qualify in pole position yet has virtually no
technical knowledge of the cars. Inevitably he crashes, but
while in hospital he manages to 'pull' his doctor Nicole
Kidman (he later married her in real life) who then proceeds
to follow him around, nursing him back to health and a win
in the Daytona 500. *Days of Thunder*, really *Top Gun* on
wheels and co-scripted by Cruise, flopped commercially.

the car's the star

without it there's nothing

FOR MOST READERS the cars are naturally the main reason for watching any of the films listed in this book. However, there are those who are even more devout in their support of their (seldom exotic) marque or model of choice: the Skoda fans who eagerly watch *North by Northwest* for the early Octavia that appears on back projection behind Cary Grant's head, or the Ford Escort owners who would actually endure *The Crucible of Terror* in order to marvel at James Bolam's blue Mk1. Such car fanatics have learned to edit video-tape so that they can compile a feature-length film of their preferred car, occasionally wondering why their neighbours tend to decline any social invitations.

So, while this chapter is not necessarily aimed at such loyal supporters of their favourite car, it is a means of including films that simply would not function on an aesthetic or dramatic level without the inclusion of a motor vehicle. On these grounds this chapter might reasonably be expected to include road movies or any film that strongly features anything with an internal combustion engine, but after much editing and refinement five sub-categories have been arrived at.

First we have the films that would bore the viewer into a coma were it not for the cars – films in which the leading actors are constantly up-staged by the products of Detroit. *Days of Thunder* must head the list, boasting as it does Tom Cruise giving his Alan Ladd-for-the-1990s performance, lots of macho posturing and the waste of Robert Duvall. The recent remake of *Gone in 60 Seconds* also comes under this heading, the crashes being a welcome distraction from acting that wouldn't pass muster in a Roger Corman epic.

Then there are the 'titular' cars, which occur across a broad sweep of celluloid genres. *The F. J. Holden* refers to Australia's developing post-war identity, *Christine* is the Plymouth from Hell and Walt Disney's *Gnome-Mobile* is a Rolls-Royce full of – well, gnomes really. Then there is *The Car*, a demonic Lincoln that prompts B-movie king James Brolin's finest ever dialogue – 'The Car is in the garage!'

Another category is where a car – sometimes an extremely mundane model – powers the narrative. For every *Yellow Rolls-Royce* or, for Belmondo fans, solid gold TR4 in *Échappement libre*, there is Richard Todd's quest for his 105E Anglia in *Never Let Go* or the 1964 Chevrolet Malibu in *Repo Man*. It may be more than one car – the 1963 Nissan Cedric and the world's least reliable Jaguar XJ6 in *The Big Steal*, or the Ford GB Press Fleet of Consul-Cortinas in *Carry On Cabby*. Films with titles such as *Car Wash* should be considered quite self-explanatory.

The next category is films that rely heavily on a chase sequence. The first half of *The Italian Job* appears to be a variant, in colour, of an early 1960s British crime-caper and, dare one suggest, would be remembered as such if it were not for the trio of Austin Mini-Cooper Ss. In a similar vein, denude *Ronin* or *The Seven-Ups* of their exceptional chase sequences, and you are left with fine actors such as Robert de Niro and Roy Schneider mouthing B-movie dialogue and looking vaguely embarrassed as they do so. This is not to deny how welcome a decent car chase can be in the midst of a particularly turgid film – if Peter Hyams's *Capricorn One* is recalled at all, it is for the suspiciously Keystone Cops-like sequence of Elliott Gould driving his brakeless Mk1 six-cylinder Mustang automatic into the drink at approximately Warp Speed 10.

Finally there is automotive pornography. Although many readers may expect *Crash* to head this category, that honour must go to the original *Gone in 60 Seconds* of 1974. This features one of the most sustained chase sequences ever filmed. It was put together by a Hollywood stuntman who didn't think actors looked natural on screen, so cast himself and his girlfriend in the leading roles. From memory they're no worse than Mr V. Jones in the remake. Every aspect of this great film – the amateurish acting, the muddy colour cinematography and the manner in which the camera lingers on each crumpled panel on every De Ville and Riviera – brings to mind certain German and Scandinavian productions of the same era in a way that makes our enthusiasm seem positively healthy. Almost.

The Adventures of Hal 5

GB, 1957, 59mins, b&w

Dir: Don Sharp

Ah the delights of the Children's Film Foundation! The timeless joys of a long-lost world where Dennis Waterman raced soapboxes and intrepid youngsters found treasure in Malta. Here, HAL 5 is a 1923 Austin 7 'Chummy' sold by spiv John Glyn-Jones to decent chap – he is a clergyman after all – William Russell. It transpires that HAL (utterly no connection to *2001: a Space Odyssey*) is in fact magic, with a mind of its own. Incidentally, there is absolutely no relationship between HAL 5 and a certain series of films featuring a magic VW Beetle. Honest.

A Spanish Affair

(aka Aventura para dos)

US/Sp, 1958, 93mins, colour

Dir: Don Siegel/Luis Marquina

One of the least revived entries in the Siegel canon, *A Spanish Affair* boasts the unusual (for a 1950s medium-budget American film) combination of colour cinematography, extensive location footage and, the prime reason for viewing, a Pegaso Z102. In fact Siegel's autobiography devotes more wordage to the car than to the leading cast members, lavishing praise on the 'Spanish Ferrari' – he ensured that the Pegaso appeared in virtually every scene. When you consider that Spain's first 'indigenous' – albeit Fiat-derived – car was launched as late as 1953, any film boasting that country's 'jewel for the rich' in its prime must be essential viewing.

Ice Cold in Alex

GB, 1958, 135mins, b&w

Dir: J. Lee Thompson

Ice Cold could have easily found a place in the 'Road Movies' chapter. The central narrative concerns four disparate characters, thrown together by circumstance (the fall of Tobruk in 1942), and crossing a bleak and alien landscape towards an apparently unattainable goal. Captain Anson of the RAMC (John Mills in a career-best performance that amazingly wasn't even Oscar nominated) is a shell-shocked alcoholic with a justifiable terror of falling into Axis hands – he was previously captured and managed to escape but is now in severe danger of going completely sand-happy. Together with his RSM (Harry Andrews) and two female nurses, he takes an Austin K2 Ambulance with the intention of making for Alexandria. The snag is that the Royal Engineers blow the road bridge to hinder the Germans, so Anson has to take the long route through the desert. All the while he dreams of ice-cold lager in his favourite bar. But will 'Katie' the ambulance stand up to the rigours of the journey? The film was shot on location in Libya and 90% of the film takes place within the Austin. Thompson's camerawork really makes you feel the shimmering heat, where the only options are to sit in the sweltering rear compartment or to ride exposed to the elements in the front.

A Weekend with Lulu

GB, 1961, 90mins, b&w

Dir: John Paddy Carstairs

Just prior to the advent of Swinging London, certain middle-class British comedies had a distressing tendency to smutty titles – *The Fast Lady* (q.v.), *A Pair of Briefs* (two barristers), *Double Bunk* (a steam vessel) and *A Weekend with Lulu*. *Lulu* was the last comedy film produced by Hammer until the top-grossing *On the Buses* in 1971, and it provides the viewer with a glimpse of holidaying in Bedford Romanies and their ilk, their duo-tone livery and integral 'Frigidaire' being as much a totem of suburban affluence as eating Argentinian steak and drinking Cyprus sherry.

Lulu herself is an icecream van converted into a Dormobile and piloted by Leslie Phillips (saviour of many a British comedy) and Bob Monkhouse. Regular viewers of British daytime television sometimes catch the early 1960s attempts to turn Mr Monkhouse into a comic leading man, but *Lulu* is the only film referred to with any affection in his autobiography.

Sylvia Syms, Harry Andrews, Anthony Quayle and John Mills with the Austin ambulance in the North African desert in *Ice Cold in Alex*.
(Photo: ABP/Pictorial Press Limited)

Russ Conway and Shirley Eaton posing sidesaddle on the seats of a Renault Floride convertible during filming for *A Weekend with Lulu*.
(Photo: Bertram Ostrer/BFI Collections)

Omar Sharif and Ingrid Bergman play hide the salami in *The Yellow Rolls-Royce* - clean Sunday afternoon entertainment on 1970s British TV.
(Photo: MGM/Pictorial Press Limited)

Bottom left: Herbie, the VW with a mind of its own, demonstrates the lift-off oversteer characteristics of swing axle rear suspension in The *Love Bug*.
(Photo: Disney/Pictorial Press Limited)

Bottom centre: American spec Mercedes 450SL gets a scrub-down from the zany employees in *Car Wash*.
(Photo: Universal/Pictorial Press Limited)

Bottom right: Orgasmic action in the poster for *The Betsy*.
(Photo: Allied Artists/Harold Robbins International/Pictorial Press Limited)

Échappement libre

Fr, 1964, 105mins, b&w

Dir: Jean Becker

With Jean-Paul Belmondo starring, Gitanes naturally play a major part – only Robert Mitchum, Humphrey Bogart and Yves Montand could smoke better. But it is our hero's method of bullion smuggling that concerns us, using the ingenious method of a solid gold TR4, which cannot have benefited its ground clearance or handling. This was apparently released before a certain 007 film that featured a gold Rolls-Royce.

The Yellow Rolls-Royce

GB, 1964, 122mins, colour

Dir: Anthony Asquith

Despite a Terence Rattigan script and a glittering cast – Rex Harrison, Shirley MacLaine, George C. Scott, Alain Delon and Ingrid Bergman – this story about the various owners of a Phantom 1 didn't turn anyone's crank and seemed curiously dated in 1964. NB: More than one RR is used – watch the spare wheel holder.

The Love Bug

US, 1968, 107mins, colour

Dir: Robert Stevenson

First and best of the *Herbie* films about the VW Beetle with a mind of its own. Good stunts, and David Tomlinson as the dastardly villain is characteristically excellent. He drives a rare Apollo sports car. Lots of other desirable machinery can be spotted in the background of the racing sequences.

Car Wash

US, 1976, 96mins, colour

Dir: Michael Schultz

Zany goings-on at the Dee-Luxe Car Wash in L.A. *Car Wash* featured comedian Richard Pryor and Antonio Fargas, better known as Huggy Bear out of TV show *Starsky and Hutch*. Bad haircuts, flared trousers and plenty of American spec Euro exotica alongside the usual yank tanks.

Confessions of a Driving Instructor

GB,1976, 90mins, colour

Dir: Norman Cohen

This film stars a midnight blue 1968 Ford Cortina Mk2 Super with a Webasto roof and a floor gearchange. There's also Robin Askwith, who shows his arse, as does Anthony 'My son-in-law is the PM' Booth. Meanwhile, William Friese-Greene revolves in his grave. A 90-minute glimpse into hell.

The F. J. Holden

Aus, 1977, 101mins, colour

Dir: Michael Thornhill

Several films in the 'Australian Cinema Revival' of the 1970s were period dramas that attempted to define an individual national identity. However, *The F. J. Holden* is fairly atypical in that it is set in the Panania district of contemporary Sydney. We meet Kev, a typically sartorially challenged youth of that period (well it was 1977), who lives for little more than his long-suffering girlfriend Anne and, naturally, drag racing his beloved 1953 FJ-Series Holden, the first all-Australian car. *The F. J. Holden* is a rites-of-passage movie rarely seen in the UK, unavailable on video but worth catching for its array of elderly vehicles – not just from Holden but a fair smattering of Lancers, Valiants, Majors and even the odd Kimberley-Six. Incidentally, some of the cast did indeed appear in *Prisoner Cell Block H* – in the late 1970s it was almost obligatory.

The Betsy

US, 1978, 100mins, colour

Dir: Daniel Petrie

Laurence Olivier is Loren Hardeman Sr, American motor magnate and classical actor with pressing debts! Tommy Lee Jones is Angelo Perino, Italian-American stud! Together with Robert Duvall and Katharine Ross, they star in this epic adaptation of Harold Robbins's novel in which everyone seems to spend an inordinate amount of time lying on the floor, wracked with orgasms. Apparently there are also cars in the story, but my celluloid nerve failed me. Sorry.

A lost and forlorn Bob Hoskins at the wheel of the Mk2 Jaguar in *Mona Lisa*. (Photo: Handmade/Pictorial Press Limited)

Jeff Bridges as Preston Tucker with a 1948 Model 48 Tucker in *Tucker: The Man and His Dream*. (Photo: UIP/Lucas Films/Pictorial Press Limited)

Mona Lisa

GB, 1986, 104mins, colour
Dir: Neil Jordan

Some of Britain's finest 'cockney' actors hail from places well out of earshot of Bow Bells – Michael Elphick (Chichester) and Sidney James (Johannesburg) to name but two. *Mona Lisa* stars Suffolk's own 'cockney' Bob Hoskins in one of Handmade Production's best films, together with *Withnail & I* (q.v.). *Mona* has our hero, George, recently released from the Scrubs and feeling totally adrift in a London of proto-yuppies. Mr Mortwell offers him the job of chauffeuring black call-girl Simone (Cathy Tyson), a job

George gladly takes as he gets to drive a white Mk2 Jaguar. The 1970s, when tarnished Mk2s lurked in the *Auto Trader* are well and truly over, and the car now commands respect in the classic car press and is considered an 'investment'. George has re-entered an England where the past is now commoditised.

Hoskins gives a masterly portrayal of George as a dubious combination of Knight Errant and Don Quixote piloting the white Mk2 through a London he no longer comprehends. The Jaguar is the very breed of car that a younger George would have coveted back in the 1960s, but *Mona Lisa* spares little room for nostalgia. Soho is rife with massage parlours, all staffed by girls of the same age as his own daughter. Controlling them is his boss the hideous Mortwell, brilliantly played by Michael Caine as Alfie Elkins gone to the bad.

Mona Lisa is far from a perfect film; Robbie Coltrane's narration is superfluous and the 'truth' about Simone is fairly well telegraphed, but Bob Hoskins's performance as an ageing mobster, increasingly taking refuge in the past to avoid the tribulations of the present, is as perfect as his mode of transport. Possibly the best use of a Mk2 in a London film since *Performance*.

Tucker:
The Man and His Dream
US, 1988, 115mins, colour
Dir: Francis Ford Coppola

Francis Ford Coppola was fascinated by Tucker cars from the moment he first saw one as a boy in the '40s. His father had been one of the people who had lost money in the Tucker stock issue. He eventually bought one and, for 10 years, nurtured a project to make a film about the car and its designer, Preston Tucker. In fact, he shares his interest in the car with George Lucas and they owned four between them when the film was made.

Tucker: The Man and His Dream is not so much about the car as about the man, although it never really explores his motivations or truly reveals his private life. It paints a Preston Tucker who is a genial, incurable optimist who gathers a small band around him and inspires them to build a car that, allegedly, frightened the established American motor industry so much with its modern features (seat belts, pop-out screen, disc brakes) that they conspired to put him out of business. Tucker – played with ever-present broad grin by Jeff Bridges – lacks common sense or any idea of the real odds against him. Living in the bosom of an apple-pie family that makes the Waltons look knowing and cynical, Tucker applies for the use of a war-surplus manufacturing plant in Chicago to build his car. The car is launched with massive publicity. Stock is issued

to raise money and he sets up his assembly line and starts racing against a deadline for introducing his first model. All looks set fair for success, but then dark forces begin to gather as the established interests manipulate the media against Tucker.

Twenty-two original Tuckers and four glass fibre replicas based on 1974 Ford chassis were used in the making of the film. The fakes are the cars without windscreen wipers. In its original form the film was three hours long, but after a preview it was felt a substantial cut was needed, and many technical scenes which it would have been good to see got axed.

The Big Steal
Aus, 1990, 99mins, colour
Dir: Nadia Tass

Young Danny Clark is an eminently sensible fellow who adores both Jaguars (an Australian fan of *Robbery* perhaps) and apparently unattainable women. Being totally broke isn't going to halt his plans, so whilst his parents are away he strikes a deal with a very obvious spiv, one Gordon Farkas, to exchange his father's immaculate 1963 Nissan Cedric for a 1974 Series 2 XJ6. The true star of the film is the 1963 Nissan Cedric 31 Series Mk1, a car with a determined cult following in Australia. The Cedric was advertised as: 'The £2,390 luxury car for £1,375.' This price tag placed the car not in the Holden/Valiant/Falcon marketplace but also ranged it against Anglo-Australians such as the locally built PB Cresta and the Wolseley 24/80. However, Cedrics were already being used as Brisbane taxis and the De-Luxe spec. offered tinted glass and a transistor radio. No wonder that Mr Clark will not be too happy at the loss of his Cedric. But, of course, Mr Farkas gets his come-uppance – the poor chap has a name straight out of a *Carry On* when we learn that he is a transvestite. So, for those readers who desire either a decent low-key comedy film or are rabid Cedric fans, *The Big Steal* is better entertainment than many a contemporary Hollywood film, despite (or maybe because of) the image of Steve Bisley in a frock.

cops & robbers

the thrill of the chase

TO BRITISH VIEWERS, a mundane American police vehicle can seem glamorous. It is not merely the size and, on occasion, the baroque tail fins that appeal, also the variety of law-enforcement agencies and officers to hand. So, even when a film-maker gives a dull vehicle to his cop, it may suggest verve. Two examples are Rod Steiger from *In The Heat of The Night* and Clint Eastwood's *Dirty Harry*. A variation on the 'hard-working cop in his hard-working Ford' routine is for a film to establish the hero's street cred yet include a fancy car chase. A police driver in *The Taking of Pelham 1-2-3* summarised such scenes: 'This is great! We're scaring the crap out of everybody!'

The French Connection establishes a 'cultured European' villain to pit against our hamburger hero. Everyone knows that any half-decent 'European' or Ivy League thief will use a Rolls-Royce or Mercedes-Benz and probably collect art. The criminal with social pretensions may adopt a mask of middle-class values – Richard Burton's Rover P5B Coupé in *Villain* or Jean Gabin's Ford Comet in *Touchez Pas au Grisbi*. Or they may opt for an uneasy blend of 'heritage' and ostentation – see the MkX Jaguars in *Gangster No.1* and *The Krays* and Stephen Boyd's Silver Shadow in *The Squeeze*. But for conspicuous consumption, any good Scorsese or Coppola epic will display wonderfully decadent cars for the mob boss of the 1940s onwards.

In post-war British films, an American (actually often Canadian) car is the spiv choice: consider the Bogarde/Doonan Buick in *The Blue Lamp*, car racketeer Peter Sellers and his fleet of Americana in *Never Let Go* or the Cadillacs in *Get Carter*. The getaway car for your monochrome British thug has to be the MkVII Jaguar, with room for six chums if you specify automatic transmission. Films such as *The Good Die Young* or *The Challenge* would be dull without a villain (black shirt, white tie) spinning the four-spoke steering wheel as the police clang behind.

And so to the cars used by Britain's finest. One marque stars. Yes, there are strong cases to be made for the Jaguar S-types in *Robbery* and *Frenzy*, the Ford Granadas, Rover P6s and Triumph 2500s in *The Sweeney* films, or the Humber Hawks and Super Snipes in *The Blue Lamp*. But none compares with the Wolseley. Until as late as 1970, police Wolseleys – sleek, black and manoeuvrable as the *Queen Mary* – patrolled Britain's streets. Actually, since many of them were the property of either Jack Silk or Joe Wadham they were usually the very same examples of 18/85, 6/80, 6/90, 6/99 or 6/110. The 6/80s in the Scotland Yard series helped to distract from Edgar Lustgarten's charisma-free presence, while the later models maintained police dignity in crime epics, the driver often ringing the gong in deserted streets to give the villains a sporting chance.

Gun Crazy
US, 1949, 85mins, b&w
Dir: Joseph H. Lewis

No book that details *Badlands, Bande à parte, Bonnie and Clyde* or *Les Valseuses* should omit *Gun Crazy*, one of America's most influential B-movies and one of the greatest films never to be nominated for an Oscar.

Ex-reformatory inmate and GI marksman John Dall teams up with English fairground sharpshooter Peggy Cummins. Lewis once remarked that he wanted their first meeting to resemble 'two dogs on heat' and this five-minute sequence informs the audience all that they need to know about the characters of the immature Dall and the calculating Cummins. They eventually marry, but money is tight and Peggy is not content to live on a $40 weekly wage, taunting Dall that he is no man unless he can provide for her. After a montage of quick hold-up sequences, in which the pair get considerable erotic satisfaction from the use of firearms, they hijack Don Beddoe's blue '49 Cadillac Sedan. Peggy poses as a lone hitch-hiker exposing much nylon-clad limb in the process, and after the unfortunate Don picks her up and attempts some really lame chat-up lines, Peggy produces a handgun from her bag and points it at Mr Beddoe's ample midriff – 'would you like to stop for a while?'

There then ensues one of the finest robbery sequences in American cinema. Lewis mounted the camera on the rear seat of the Cadillac and the entire 210-second sequence is shot from this viewpoint. As the couple verbally work themselves up to commit the robbery – equating with sexual foreplay – Peggy parks the car in front of a downtown bank and engages passing cop Robert Osterloh in conversation. As soon as John emerges, she karate-chops the unlucky plod and the duo career off, taking the Cadillac around seemingly impossible corners and honking at all passers-by.

Dumping the Cadillac by its bound and gagged owner, they flee in their own Chevrolet. But time is running out. Even if they do manage to pass through a police roadblock by dressing as respectable and bespectacled citizens, their next stick-up leads to the State Troopers pursuing the Chevrolet in their screaming black and white Dodge. Dall manages to shoot out the police car tyres as our anti-heroes cross the state line. After this he is all for retiring from criminal life. Peggy, however, wants just one last job.

Thus, a few months later we see John and Peggy as eminently dull employees of a Montana meatpacking factory; he as a truck driver, she as a secretary, the better to plan a payroll heist. They escape in their Chevrolet intending to dump it and finally separate. But the couple is now as inextricably doomed as the Macbeths, and Lewis shows both getaway cars head off and U-turn towards each other. The final shoot-out is less than two reels away.

Gun Crazy, also known as *Deadly is the Female*, was co-scripted by the author of the original story, MacKinlay Kantor, with the blacklisted Dalton Trumbo (writing as Millard Kaufman). It contains sharp period detail, from the inspection of cars for fruit and vegetables at the Californian state line to the seedy diners where the duo scrape together the funds for hamburger with onion. The cinematography is exceptional.

The Blue Lamp
GB, 1950, 84mins, b&w
Dir: Basil Dearden

'They've found the bastard that killed George Dixon.' *Dixon of Dock Green* was an amiable bobby whose BBC adventures in and around a Paddington Police Station dominated Saturday evening TV between 1955 and 1976. There are some cynics who wondered if George Dixon had committed some terrible *faux pas* early in his career, given that he wasn't made a Sergeant until he was 68, but the very name George Dixon is still shorthand for the traditional copper armed only with a whistle chain. Yet few know of the film that spawned the character – *The Blue Lamp*, one of the best pieces of publicity ever devised for the London Metropolitan Police.

Basil Dearden establishes from the outset that this is an Ealing drama in the wartime documentary mode. There is no theme music to the opening credits – save for the Winkworth on a police Humber Super Snipe. The front grille of the Rootes Group's finest fills the screen as the squad car speeds through the bomb-scarred streets of West London. The city is undergoing a crime wave. The front line against such villainy is exemplified by the middle-aged PC George Dixon (Jack Warner) and the probationer Andy Mitchell (Jimmy Hanley), a responsible lad who sports wartime campaign medals on his tunic. Ranged against them are two wideboys, Tom Riley (Dirk Bogarde) and Spud (Patric Doonan), who are far too irresponsible to join the official London underworld – they both sport zoot suits with hand-painted ties, and drive a 1937 Buick drophead.

Up until the halfway mark, the film carefully contrasts the warm community values of the Dock Green station with the seedy milieu of Spud and Tom – all peeling lodging houses and purloined revolvers. The shooting of Dixon by Riley is the apex of the narrative – there will be no hiding place for one who dares disturb the Ealing *status quo*. The dragnet tightens and the transgressors flee, and here the pace visibly quickens. The Radio Control Room at the Yard

A post-war London villain's failed getaway in a rare six-cylinder MG, pursued by a Police Humber, in Basil Dearden's *The Blue Lamp*. (Photo: Rank/Dr Steven Chibnall Collection)

is galvanised into action, dispatching flotillas of Super Snipes and 18/85s. According to Warner's autobiography, many of the cars (and crews) were the genuine Met article, and Dearden's direction of the chase easily compares to any product of Hollywood. The Super Snipe was one of the few British cars to compete with American vehicles for Empire sales, its vast 4-litre engine and excellent ground clearance being as suitable for the Australian outback as for policing the mother country. Meanwhile, the Wolseley 18/85, a car beloved of British officialdom until as late as 1957, blocks any retreat. But, calamity! A schoolmistress is herding a crocodile of schoolgirls across the road; the Humber nearly annihilates the lot before skidding to a halt. More than half a century later it is almost impossible to imagine having to stop nearly two tons of speeding leather and walnut without a brake servo, let alone ABS. Incidentally, this sequence was brilliantly replayed in 1967 by Peter Yates in *Robbery*. Many of the same locations were used for the chase sequence in West London.

Spud is killed when the Buick (inevitably) crashes. The police and the underworld communities, working in league, catch Tom, and the film ends with Andy Mitchell carrying on Dixon's good work. Both Sir Harold Nicholson, London's Police Commissioner, and most British film critics were delighted with this fusion of American docudrama (*The Naked City*), post-war spiv drama and Ealing community values. The cinematic legacy of *The Blue Lamp* would be felt in Britain in terms of policiers until the late 1960s despite the one British critic who bemoaned 'the spurious attempts at characterisation'. But no one else seemed to notice that by making police officers paragons of virtue, they might actually be doing the force a disfavour – Dixon's humanity owes more to Warner's considerable acting talents than to the screenplay. Furthermore, even if Tom Riley is sent to the gallows, the sexually charged performance of Dirk Bogarde hinted at a romantic/decadent strain of British cinema that would resurface with a vengeance by the end of the decade. But for the moment, Wolseley-driven values triumphed.

Touchez Pas au Grisbi
aka Hands off the loot and Honour among Thieves
Fr, 1953, 94mins, b&w
Dir: Jacques Becker

Max le menteur (Jean Gabin) is a successful gangster-about-town. A silver-haired bachelor with a sharp line in suits, Max carries a world-weary air, too tired to even make love to Jeanne Moreau. No, he merely wishes to spend his autumn years eating and drinking of the very finest, listening to melancholic harmonica strains and cruising the Parisian boulevards in his '52 Ford V8 Veddette. The French-built Ford, derided by the bourgeoisie as *Un Voiture de Nouveau Riche*, is actually the ideal transport for a respectable mobster, given that the Citroën 15CV was approaching the end of its run and the Renault Fregate suffered from Vanguarditis. His 2i/c 'Riton' is aged in his 50s and favours petit-bourgeois respectability in the forms of a toothbrush moustache and a Simca Aronde. To fund their retirement, they have pulled off one final bullion heist but the Italian-tailored young turk Angelo (Lino Ventura in his film debut) is waiting to muscle in on their territory.

The gangs of Max and Angelo conduct their nocturnal business untroubled by the Gendarmerie. Dispatching their emissaries in Onze Legres, the final confrontation is in deserted woodland. Using a choice selection of Delages and Delahayes – both hoods have far better taste than your Soho mobster – the shootout leads to the destruction of the loot (the grisbi) and the death of Riton.

The Good Die Young
GB, 1954, 100mins, b&w
Dir: Lewis Gilbert

The opening credits establish the British film noir sensibility with the good – broke former GI Richard Basehart, cuckolded USAF Sergeant John Ireland and crippled boxer Stanley Baker – being driven by unspeakably camp playboy Laurence Harvey in a stolen MkVII Jaguar through the mean streets of London. After all, if you're going to commit a bullion heist, the correct car is *de rigueur*. The other motoring note is struck by the boyfriend of Mrs John Ireland in a white Jowett Jupiter no less. Do they get away with it? Of course not: this is still 1954.

The Long Arm

GB, 1956, 96mins, b&w

Dir: Charles Frend

'This looks like blood,' observes Det.-Supt. Halliday as he scrapes at the radiator grille of a V8 Pilot. Jack Hawkins's quiet delivery of these words entirely changes the tone of the scene. Previously we had seen car dealer Harry Locke being sold a fog lamp by two urchins with taxi-door ears. Suspicious, as the lamp is new, he calls PC Nicholas Parsons. The boys confess – it came from a Pilot in a scrapyard. The Super and Det.-Sgt. Ward (John Stratton) are called: could this be the car that ran over a night watchman?

The Long Arm was the final film to be produced at Ealing's studios and follows in the tradition of *The Blue Lamp* – tireless police force protecting the community. But five years after George Dixon's debut, the pressures are seen to be greater; admittedly he holds a far more senior rank but the constraints of his role do not allow for any home life. This film is far more low-key – unusually for a 1950s British policier there is barely a clang from a Winkworth and certainly no chases. The 6/80 seen immediately post-credits is an unmarked Q-car ('the area car was away, chasing teddy boys,' explains the driver) investigating a break-in. It's obviously an inside job, but since the main suspect, Sydney Tafler, is so wonderfully spivvy, he must be ruled out. The investigation makes no headway until young night watchman Ian Bannen attempts to stop a suspicious Ford Pilot.

There are certain films that make an indelible impression on the juvenile mind, and the sight of the Pilot's massive headlamps bearing down upon the unfortunate Mr Bannen gave me nightmares. Bannen survives just long enough to respond to Hawkins's questioning – 'Was it big? Was it dark? Was it a saloon?' – to make Halliday and Ward give the Ford the once-over at the scrapyard. From this point, the narrative acquires pace, climaxing with Hawkins attempting to halt the Triumph 2000 Roadster belonging to the villain's moll by clinging to the bonnet. Round and round she speeds through the Festival Hall car park until Hawkins risks life and limb by shattering the windscreen with his police truncheon. Justice prevails in a solidly well-made crime film that bears comparison with *Hell is a City* made only three years later.

Hell is a City

GB, 1959, 95mins, b&w

Dir: Val Guest

Night in a British city. All decent citizens are safe at home, listening to the Home Service and sipping cocoa, but to keep the mean streets free of low-life a Series III Wolseley 6/90 patrols through the darkness to the insistent beat of a high-hat cymbal. The camera cuts to a POV shot through the police-car windscreen and, as the saxophones wail, the credit flashes up – *Hell is a City*.

A good credit sequence is worth its weight in gold to any film – it can certainly be the saviour of a bad one (*Walk On The Wild Side* anyone?) – but the opening of *Hell is a City* establishes that here is a British crime movie that, aside from the Wolseley, owes more to a 1940s Hollywood film noir. It concerns the efforts of Detective-Inspector Harry Martineau (Stanley Baker) of Manchester CID to recapture escaped murderer Don Starling (Jon Crawford). Professionally the Inspector seems eminently satisfied: he has achieved his rank at quite a young age, is a feared/respected man about town and has the use of an unmarked 6/90 and an eager young assistant. His private life is disastrous, however. He shuns his semi and chases Starling instead.

The fact that Val Guest directed *Confessions of a Window Cleaner* should not obscure the quality of his 1950s and 1960s work, all of which demonstrated imaginative location filming. The police Wolseleys and Austin A95s in

Hell were the genuine article – as were many of the uniformed PCs playing bit parts. The supporting cast is faultless, their choice of cars reflecting their personae. Take Warren Mitchell's commercial traveller who discovers the corpse of the bookmaker's secretary. He is very fussy and sports a bow-tie, so obviously his Morris Oxford Series III would be decked out in fog lamps and car club badges – all proof of his generous commission. The bookmaker, played by Donald Pleasence, is a mix of shrewdness, cynicism and genuine affection for his flighty young wife. A Ford Consul De Luxe Mk2 Estate is perfect for him – more economical and practical than a Zephyr-Six saloon but with the leather seats and duotone paint of a Zodiac. Best of all is the 1938 Canadian-built Buick chosen by Starling and his gang when doing the robbery. This isn't a slick London firm with a MkVIII Jaguar and a tame lawyer; these are seedy provincial villains with a £25 getaway car probably acquired from a bombsite dealer.

Guest's camera records a Manchester that is fast leaving the vestiges of wartime behind it; the city's taxis are A55/Oxford Farinas as early as 1959 and the streets are full of recent model Victors and Minxes.

Come the final reel and Starling has been sent to the gallows. Baker sheds a manly tear, attempts to be reasonable to his wife and walks out into the streets of Manchester. Now a DCI, he greets his former partner as their CID Wolseley is called off on yet another job. Cue the closing credits, with the POV shot of the city at night, changing to the camera tracking away from the speeding 6/90 as the legend 'The End' flashes up. With such drama, it would be churlish to note that the police-car in the credit sequence has a Middlesex number plate and London Met livery.

Don Siegel fans who believe all b&w British crime movies with a Wolseley are B-movies might give *Hell is a City* a try. This is the film that allegedly caused apoplexy in Manchester's Chief Constable when he saw a preview – in 1959 Inspectors never threatened suspects, argued with their wives or lusted after barmaids.

The Man in the Back Seat
GB, 1960, 57mins, b&w
Dir: Vernon Sewell

Very few British second-features seem worth setting the VCR timer for. Naturally there are the delights of acting so stilted that the performers are under Forestry Commission protection, flexible scenery and direction that makes Gerald Thomas appear an auteur in comparison. However, for genuinely gripping narratives, Vernon Sewell directed several supernatural and crime thrillers for Independent Artists, one of the best-remembered being *The Man in the Back Seat*.

The plot is economical: two young men hijack a bookie and steal his car. Then their troubles start – the bookie might have been injured during the kidnap, his assailants cannot separate him from his cash bag, and they squabble as to how they can leave him at a hospital without arousing police suspicion. Virtually all the narrative takes place within the victim's car, which is the reason for including the film: our turf accountant drives an Austin A125 Sheerline. The Sheerline was Austin's own interpretation of the R-Type/MkVI Bentley, launched in 1947 and immediately appealing to Birmingham industrialists and medium-sized mayoralties.

As played by Derren Nesbitt (an icon of British B-movies) and Keith Faulkner, 'Tony' and 'Frank' aren't nasty teddy boys but panicking young men. They fend off approaches from a police 6/90 and an AA patrolman in his Land Rover, but the presence of the dead or comatose Harry Locke ('Joe Carter' the bookie) on the back seat increasingly unnerves them – his silent presence seems accusatory. Just before the final reel they decide to return to the dog-track. In his rear-view mirror, Frank seems to see Harry sit bolt upright (shades of the Scottish play) – so unnerving him that he crashes. The big Austin explodes.

The Man in the Back Seat, with *Strongroom* and *The House of Mystery*, are British second-features at their very best, using budgetary limitations to evoke a horribly claustrophobic world. Forget *The Car* – Vernon Sewell makes a far better ghost story on 10% of the budget and using only a second-hand Austin.

An AA man tells Keith Faulkner that his A125 has hydraulic jacks, in *The Man in the Back Seat*. *(Photo: Independent Artists/Pictorial Press Limited)*

cars in films

Payroll
GB, 1961, 94mins, b&w
Dir: Sidney Hayers

Hayers mainly directed ITV dramas and British second-features but this surprisingly hard-hitting piece is a definite A-movie. Mainly shot on location on Tyneside, it has ruthless young gang boss Michael Craig, his psychotic Liverpudlian 2i/c Tom Bell (excellent performance) plus rank-and-filers Barry Keegan and Kenneth Griffith in their Type 1 VW van tailing bank messengers in a MkVIa Super Snipe. The sudden appearance of a motorcycle cop puts paid to that effort, so the gang next concentrate on William Peacock's security van. In a tense and violent sequence, Keegan rams it with his Thames Trader, breaking the security guard's neck. The gang flee in a Mk1 Jaguar 3.4 and a MkII Zodiac, but it is just a matter of time before they are caught, either through their own squabbling, the efforts of vengeful widow Billie Whitelaw and Inspector Andrew Faulds, or via their contact man William Lucas, a snivelling emasculated accountant with a 103A Popular. The film is so well paced that it takes a while to notice that no-one seems to have a Geordie accent. Craig is a much better hood than a lightweight Rank leading man.

Branded to Kill
(aka Koroshi no rakuin)
Jap, 1967, 98mins, b&w
Dir: Seijun Suzuki

Hanada Goro is ace No. 3 hit man for the Yazuka. All he requires from life is to sniff boiled rice in order to achieve sexual satisfaction and to become hit man No. 1 (any resemblance between the works of Suzuki and Patrick McGoohan are apparently coincidental). But when a butterfly alights on his gun barrel, Hanada botches a job ...

This is about as coherent a summary as is possible of *Branded to Kill*'s plot, boasting as it does naked nymphomaniacs, enigmatic dialogue and rather a lot of rice sniffing – all filmed in glossy b&w stock. Although the higher echelons of the Yazuka favour imported gajin cars –

Mercedes-Benz 220SE Fintails or 1958 Bel Airs – poor No. 3 escapes in a Japanese-built Renault 4CV and endures a shoot-out in a dried river bed while piloting a Morris Minor 1000 – a bizarre image made all the more poignant as the Japanese motor-industry overtook the UK's in 1966.

Branded to Kill helped to gain Suzuki his dismissal from his studio – apparently they'd wanted a pot-boiler. By 1967 he had already made a gangster picture involving a gay knitting circle (*Akutaro*) and a pop-art Yazuka epic in which the hero persistently sings the theme song at inopportune moments (*Tokyo Drifter*). *Branded to Kill* does surface on *Film Four* and is unmissable for supporters of Lynch, Woo, Walters, Gilliam or indeed anyone who wants to see a real cult movie.

Point Blank
US, 1967, 92min, colour
Dir: John Boorman

The vehicular cast is all-American in this British-directed story of a gangster (Lee Marvin) taking revenge on a former friend (John Vernon) who cheats him out of stolen money, shoots him, leaves him for dead and then steals his girlfriend. Violent, with realistic fights, the Los Angeles landscape of *Point Blank* is brightly lit and brutally concrete – big office blocks and storm drains. The best scene is where Marvin takes a test drive in a used Imperial convertible, ramming it into concrete pylons at high speed in order to frighten information out of a greasy car dealer. Another memorable car is a black Dodge Charger, the original more angular type then just about to be replaced.

Robbery
GB, 1967, 108mins, colour
Dir: Peter Yates

Robbery opens with perhaps the first realistic car chase ever filmed in the UK. The actors seemed irrelevant as the real stars were the two Jaguar saloons: for the villains a silver grey Mk2 and for the police a dark blue S-type. *Robbery* was one of a handful of movies based around the

The final rumble at the villains' hideout in *Robbery*. Inspector James Booth smirks, bottom left. *(Photo: Joseph E. Levine/Oakhurst/BFI Stills, Posters and Designs)*

Great Train Robbery of 1963, others being the 1967 German docudrama *The Great British Train Robbery* and 1966's unspeakable *The Great St Trinian's Train Robbery*. In *Robbery*, names and events were altered to avoid legal action as one of the real-life train robbers – Bruce Reynolds – had yet to be caught and Ronnie Biggs was still on the run after his 1965 escape.

The film was produced by its star Stanley Baker. In his day, Baker was somewhat of a gangster groupie, hanging out with Soho face Albert Dimes (on whom he based his performance in *The Criminal*) and the train robbers. He also numbered 'Mad' Frankie Fraser among his pals. Peter Yates was hired to direct; his previous credits including *Summer Holiday* – somewhat less than anarchic but still Britain's first 'road movie'. The crash which opens *Robbery* takes place off Holborn, London, when a gas canister goes off inside a VDPS 4-litre R. Its occupants, a diamond merchant and his chauffeur, pass out and the VDP interfaces with a skip. The felons dressed as ambulance men, whisk the two men off in their stolen Austin LD30 and part the diamond geezer from his stones. They transfer themselves and the loot into the Mk2 but are then spotted by a Met Area Car – the S-type.

A high-octane pursuit ensues through relatively deserted '60s London, some of the areas being recognisable but not necessarily neighbours as shown. The chase jumps from King's Cross to Little Venice to Queensway via Notting Hill and Lancaster Gate but you don't really care because the cars keep you enthralled. There is a real sense of speed plus all the right noises – the hard snarl of the XK engine and the shrill whine of the Moss gearbox in the Mk2 makes the hairs on your neck rise. The villains jump out at high speed – look out for some appalling sound track synchronisation at this point – and disappear into the back streets, leaving the two cars dicing on the cobbled roads of what appears to be King's Cross. On cross-ply rubber neither Jaguar has much grip and the more softly suspended S-type ends up in a wild fishtail.

Packed with squealing tyres, shouting men and terrified

schoolgirls, this was the best chase in a British crime drama since *The Blue Lamp*. Steve McQueen insisted Yates direct his next film *Bullitt*.

After this first reel, could the rest of *Robbery* possibly live up to its opening? Yes, particularly if you like spotting cars and British character actors. The villains are not B-film wideboys but tailors and garage-owners with midnight blue Healeys and canary yellow E-types. Baker, as their leader, uses his own S3 and there is a strong BMC presence. There are the ambulance and VDP R, also the train heist vehicles – Austin Mini pick-up, A110 saloon, two Gypsies and a Morris J4 – not to mention Inspector James Booth's Morris Cooper Mk1. Also, take a close look at the station lookout man in the Austin Landcrab – it is Mike '*Randall and Hopkirk (Deceased)*' Pratt. George Sewell is there, of course, with Frank Finlay, Glynn Edwards, a very young Robert Powell, Ivor Dean (Inspector Teal from *The Saint*), Barry Stanton and Frank Williams (Rev. Farthing from *Dad's Army*). There are also glimpses of a Leicester Constabulary Mk2 plus a brace of police MkIV Zephyrs. These last two are not in the chase, which is possibly for the best.

Bullitt
US, 1968, 113mins, colour
Dir: Peter Yates

There isn't much left to say about *Bullitt*. Its 13-minute car chase through San Francisco is still the prototype for all the others and, arguably, it has not been bettered – although many have tried. Based on a book by Robert L. Pike (published as *Mute Witness*) this is the story of a cop (Frank Bullitt) who covers up the death of an underworld witness in his charge and goes after the killers himself.

Curiously, neither its star Steve McQueen nor its director Peter Yates wanted the chase. 'Steve had done the chase in *The Great Escape* ...' Yates told *Uncut* in 1998, '... and I'd done the chase in *Robbery*, so we weren't that keen at first.' But once the sequence was in the script both agreed that it should be the hottest ever filmed.

Although *Bullitt* now seems, vehicular action apart, like a

STEVE McQUEEN
AS 'BULLITT', AA
A SOLAR PRODUCTION

ROBERT VAUGHN

JACQUELINE BISSET · DON GORDON · ROBERT DUVALL · SIMON OAKLAND · NORMAN FELL

Directed by PETER YATES · Produced by PHILIP D'ANTONI · Executive Producer ROBERT E. RELYEA Music by Lalo Schifrin
Screenplay by ALAN R. TRUSTMAN and HARRY KLEINER • Based on the novel "Mute Witness" by Robert L. Pike

TECHNICOLOR · From WARNER BROS. Released through Warner-Pathe

Top: Steve McQueen's Mustang speeding through San Francisco in *Bullitt*. *(Photo: Warner/Solar/BFI)*

Bottom: Production shot from *Bullitt*, showing lights being set-up on McQueen's Mustang. *(Photo: Warner/Solar/Pictorial Press Limited)*

pretty routine cop drama, the fact that it was shot on location set it apart. To get a rough, documentary feel much of it was filmed using hand-held Arriflex cameras.

Nearly all the cars used are Fords, because the studio had a deal with them. The Sunshine Cab driven by Robert Duvall is a '67 Ford Custom and Robert Vaughn's transport is a black Lincoln Continental, product of the FoMoCo. Most of the police cars were Fords. Ford supplied two Highland Green Mustang 390GT fastbacks. The two black Dodge Chargers were bought by the production company from a Los Angeles dealer. While the Dodge remained in virtually standard condition, the Mustangs, because of their marginal underpinnings, had to be heavily beefed-up to endure the jumps and general abuse of the chase scene. Some tuning to the Mustang's 390ci High Performance engine was needed, apparently, to help it keep up with the Dodge's 440ci Magnum.

The chase scene took two weeks to shoot. Max Balchowski, a well-known racecar builder, was hired to keep the cars running and to do any last-minute modifications. In one downhill landing, the Mustang's oil pan was ripped open. Balchowski simply welded the pan while it was still bolted to the engine.

According to *Bullitt* aficionado Dave Kunz, McQueen did some of the stunt driving, but the tricky stuff was left to professional stunt drivers. 'When McQueen appears in the mirror, that's a good indication,' says Kunz. 'However, when the mirror is turned slightly away, and all you can see is part of the camera support, it is likely a stunt driver.'

The chase begins on Columbus Avenue in San Francisco. Bill Hickman – the character in the Charger with the horn-rimmed glasses, a top stunt driver of the day who had small speaking parts in *The French Connection* and *The Seven-Ups* – buckles his seatbelt in anticipation of jumping the lights and blasting through the junction with tyres smoking up Chestnut Street. The Mustang, caught in the traffic, finally breaks through with McQueen, rocketing up Chestnut after the Charger: the neck hairs still bristle with the sound of the V8 being gunned and anticipation of the chase, no matter how many times one sees it.

Yates wanted McQueen's Mustang to make a sharp left-hand turn from Taylor Street onto Filbert Street. As he went into the corner, the car bounced up, and he lost control, causing the Mustang to skid across the junction, according to eye-witness Anthony Bologna. After two attempts McQueen exchanged places with his stunt double who also had problems. The steep gradient forced the driver to hug the kerb in order to complete the turn. The Charger rounded the corner by oversteering sideways, then accelerating coming out. This one segment of the film is just a few seconds of screen time but took two days to film.

Bud Ekins, a great friend of McQueen's (he rode the fence jumps in *The Great Escape*) drove the downhill jumps in *Bullitt*. He also lays down a motorcycle later on in the chase when the Charger crosses the centre line and runs him off the road. At one point in the *Bullitt* chase, Hickman actually lost control of the Charger and smashes into a camera position: the final cut shows the Charger rounding the turn at Leavenworth and Chestnut, then clouting the camera at speed.

McQueen and the stunt drivers were touching 110mph in places, with Yates strapped in the back with the hand held camera. 'It was pretty terrifying,' Yates told Allan Jones in *Uncut*. 'McQueen was really flying. I eventually tapped him on the shoulder and shouted "OK you can slow down now, we're out of film." Steve turned to me and smiled. "That's nothing baby; we're also out of brakes."'

After a side-by-side game of push and shove on the open highway Bill Hickman's white haired passenger produces a sawn-off shot gun and opens fire on McQueen through the pillar-less side window of the black Dodge.

The Charger is finally consumed in a ball of fire when McQueen forces it off the road. The special-effects department built a fake service station on a vacant lot at the bottom of the hill on Guadalupe Canyon Road in Daly City, where the pursuit climaxes. The Mustang and Charger were held together by a bracket to keep the cars separated while being towed. It was then intended that the

Charger would be released, exploding as it went through the service station. In reality, the Charger missed its mark and went alongside the service station – but the explosives were set-off anyway and some nifty editing saved the scene.

Jacqueline Bissett provides McQueen's love interest. As an interesting European type she drives a slightly tatty Porsche 356.

Two bits of *Bullitt* car trivia. Look carefully in the opening part of the film in the underground car park scenes and you'll spot a Bizzarini GT Strada – one of only 149 made – parked casually among the yank tanks. When McQueen meets politico Robert Vaughn at a posh society party, linger a while on the Silver Cloud III parked outside: it's on English number plates.

Performance
GB, 1970, 105mins, colour
Dir: Nicholas Roeg, Donald Cammell

Now regarded as a classic moment in British film making, *Performance* was an embarrassment for Warner Brothers executives. They wanted another *Hard Day's Night* but got one of the darkest pieces imaginable – a dense blend of violence, murder, drugs, sado-masochism, and sex scenes so authentic (they really were having sex) as to verge on pornography. The box-office draw was Mick Jagger, but he didn't put in an appearance until 40 minutes into the plot, which was basically the story of a violent out-of-date young London gangster, Chas (James Fox), who goes on the run after murdering a bookie. He hides out with reclusive burned-out pop star Turner (Jagger) in a big house in a very pre-yuppie Notting Hill. Chas is fed some psychedelic mushrooms by Turner's mistress (Anita Pallenberg) causing him to explore more feminine areas of his personality.

Such is the cultish appeal of *Performance* that it inspired half a dozen books, yet at the time it only received a half-hearted, heavily cut release and wasn't given a proper airing until 1977.

But where do cars figure in all this? Well, the Chas/Fox character drives a white Mk2 Jaguar which fits well with the sharp suits, camel-hair overcoats, and short swept-back hairdo that made the man so out-of-step with the hippie culture of the time. He drives through a London that is a quiet place of secluded back alleys on the wrong side of the river: it's hard to believe this is the same city as that in which Lew Grade was making *Crossplot*. Notting Hill is scruffy and populated mostly with wrecks, not the latest German luxury cars.

Collecting protection money, Chas is driven around by John Binden (a genuine gangster who dabbled in acting) in a green Rover coupé, a P5 3-litre, which interestingly is fitted with P5B Rostyle wheels to make it look more up to date. A Phantom V limousine features in the opening scenes and then again when Chas and his henchmen drench it in paint, strip and shave the head of its luckless chauffeur. It appears again at the end of the film, repainted white, when Chas is being taken away to be disposed of by his gangster boss.

This is a film everyone should see. It captures the moment perfectly as the ideals of the '60s begin to yield to the darker more uncertain '70s.

Assault
GB, 1971, 91mins, colour
Dir: Sidney Hayers

Why has Chief Supt. John Velyan (Frank Finlay) been allocated an eight-year-old 6/110 as his staff car? Could he be the only senior officer who isn't on the square?

The French Connection
US, 1971, 104mins, colour
Dir: William Friedkin

Some say *The French Connection* car chase is better than the legendary one in *Bullitt*. Certainly it was grittier, swapping the clean brightly lit boulevards of San Francisco for the grimy underbelly of Brooklyn. There are no throbbing muscle cars here, just a random brown Pontiac Le Mans sedan racing a subway train under the elevated section of

James Fox pouring something corrosive on the Phantom V while the chauffeur gets a roughing over from John Binden in *Performance*. *(Photo: Warner/BFI Collections)*

Gene Hackman requisitioning a Pontiac Le Mans for the train chase in *The French Connection*. *(Photo: 20th Century Fox/Pictorial Press Limited)*

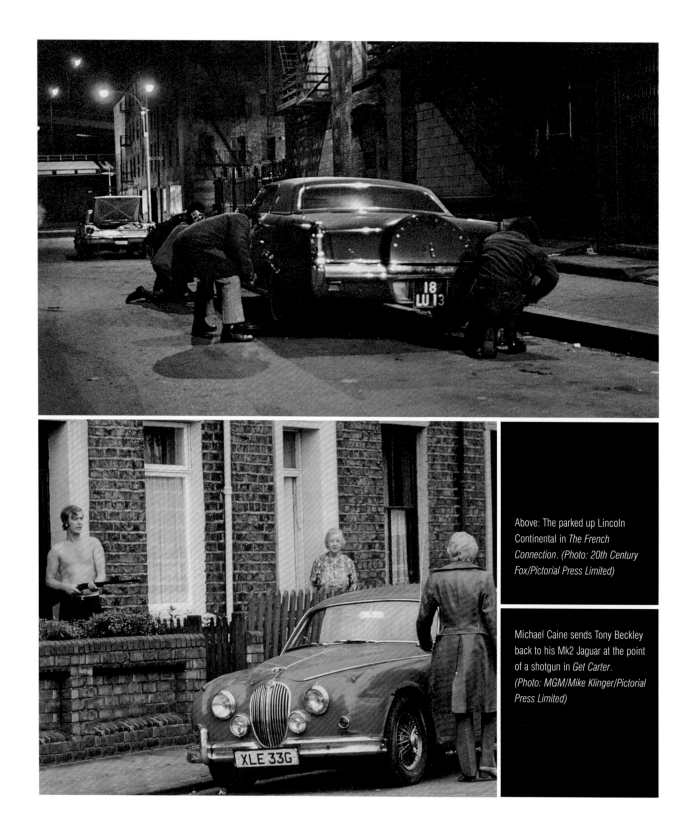

Above: The parked up Lincoln Continental in *The French Connection*. (Photo: 20th Century Fox/Pictorial Press Limited)

Michael Caine sends Tony Beckley back to his Mk2 Jaguar at the point of a shotgun in *Get Carter*. (Photo: MGM/Mike Klinger/Pictorial Press Limited)

the track. On the train is a hitman who has tried to shoot our hero. As a driver, detective Jimmy 'Popeye' Doyle (Gene Hackman) is as ordinary as his car, and in a superb sequence of editing we see him slew the lumbering machine around pedestrians, the pillars that support the track and all manner of other vehicles that lurch unwittingly into his path. Legend has it that the lady with the pram who he almost collects on his bonnet is a real member of the public, and that the Director, a youthful William Friedkin, shot the scene on unclosed roads with punters wandering about everywhere. Whatever, it was the best part of a great film which won five Oscars – Best film, Best Actor (Hackman) Best Director, Best Editing and Best Writing. Look also for the French-registered Lincoln Continental III of drug Baron Fernando Ray which is stripped down to a husk. Incidentally, there are other strong links between *The French Connection* and *Bullitt*. Producer Philip D'Antoni worked on both films. And can you spot Bill Hickman, the Charger driver from *Bullitt*, who plays a cop called Phil?

Get Carter

GB, 1971, 112mins, colour
Dir: Mike Hodges

Get Carter was based on the Ted Lewis novel *Jack's Return Home* and is an intricate tail of sex, drugs, violence and pornography that repulsed many critics on its release and attracted only modest audience numbers. It gained a subsequent cult following in the ghetto of late-night TV, although in a severely cut form, and is now regarded as an absolute classic, its gritty landscapes and cold brutality ushering in a wave of bleaker, more cynical '70s crime films. Director Mike Hodges relocated the plot from Doncaster to the more visually arresting Newcastle, inspired by the details of a real life murder case in the area. Michael Caine is Jack Carter, a professional hit man from London who returns to his native Newcastle to avenge the death of his brother in a suspicious drunken accident behind the wheel of an Austin A105 Vanden Plas. Caine now had the chance to portray a man with no redeeming features: even his black

sense of humour only allows Carter to kill with a smile.

The film is strewn with interesting cars, although Carter himself travels to Newcastle by British Rail (on a 'Deltic', then the world's most powerful diesel locomotive) and drives a hired silver MkII Cortina De Luxe. Tony Beckley (Peter) and George Sewell (Con McCarty) are dispatched by Carter's underworld bosses – the Kray-inspired Fletchers – to bring him back to London in a red Mk2 Jaguar (which is running 'G' 1969 number plates that don't tally with the specification of the car). Thorpey (Bernard Hepton) asks Carter if he might like to take up the offer of a ride to the station in his Series IV Humber Super Snipe. Local hoodlum Cyril Kinnear (John Osborne) owns a pair of '65 Cadillac Fleetwoods driven by shifty sidekick Eric Paice (Ian Hendry). It seems likely that at least one of these cars was owned by the film's producer Michael Klinger who, like the Fletchers, made his fortune in porn. Assorted heavies travel by long-wheelbase petrol-engined Land Rover SII, a vehicle that appears throughout the film.

Local fruit machine tycoon Cliff Brumby (Bryan Moseley) owns a Mulliner Park Ward Rolls-Royce Silver Shadow drophead: we see him arrive home early and cut short his daughter's party of long-haired revellers drunk on Watney's 'Party Seven'. One of them owns a Bond Bug. Glenda – Geraldine Moffat – is the girlfriend of both Brumby and Kinnear and drives a white Sunbeam Alpine. She rescues Caine from his London friends and drives him vigorously up the Gateshead multi-storey to a meeting with Brumby, who is building a restaurant on the roof. In time the plump businessman will meet a gruesome end when he's thrown from the building by Carter and lands on the bonnet of a MkIII Zephyr. Later Carter beds Glenda and learns some unsavoury home truths about his niece (or possibly daughter) Doreen. He bundles Glenda into the boot of the Alpine. In the midst of a shoot-out with Peter and Con the Alpine is nudged off a quay into the water with Glenda still inspecting the toolkit inside.

The plot of *Get Carter* is somewhat impenetrable and you tend to pick-up new details and twists at every viewing.

Villain

GB, 1971, 98mins, colour

Dir: Michael Tuchner

The critics vilified *Villain* when it appeared, condemning the violence. It has always been in the shadow of *Get Carter* mainly because the star, Richard Burton, gives an overstated 'actorish' performance while Caine, doing little, has more menace. *Villain* plots the downfall of a West London hoodlum who loves his dear old mum but gets sexual kicks out of beating up his boyfriend (Ian 'Lovejoy' McShane). Cars are part of the landscape as the action moves from the West End to the wastelands of Bracknell. Here a violent payroll robbery takes place: the hoods ram the company Vanden Plas 3-litre with a MkIV Zodiac, then T-bone it with a stolen S-type Jaguar in which they make a noisy getaway because of a fractured exhaust and flat tyres. A second Zodiac is commandeered with Joss Ackland by now bleeding all over the leather (it was an Executive) upholstery. 'Get his 'ed down, it's covered in claret' is all the sympathy Burton can muster. The choice of a Rover 3.5 coupé as Burton's official transport is significant: it was a dated car, reflecting the dated values of its owner and his wish for respectability. (Reggie Kray drove a Mercedes saloon.)

Fear is the Key

US, 1972, 108mins, colour

Dir: Michael Tuchner

Barry Newman specialised in car chases for a while in the early '70s. First there was *Vanishing Point*, then a Euro-drama called *The Salzburg Connection* and this adaptation of an Alistair MacLean novel about a man avenging the death of his wife and family in a plane crash. In the book, set in the 1950s, the hero drives a Studebaker Champion. On film it's a Ford Torino Coupé, an earlier version of the model that featured in *Starsky and Hutch*. The chase is pretty wild and comes at the start of the film so you don't have to sit through the next 100 minutes. Roy Budd, who composed the superb *Get Carter* sound track, takes credit for the music.

Frenzy

GB, 1972, colour, 116 min

Dir: Alfred Hitchcock

Frenzy is perhaps the least impressive of Hitchcock's films. It seems to be set in London of the '50s and shows Covent Garden as it used to be. Highlights include Jack Silk driving his white S-type Jaguar police car, and the scene in the back of the Commer potato lorry where the murderer struggles to extract the incriminating tie pin from the clenched fist of a woman he has just strangled: the engine noise is the genuine and unmistakable sound of a Commer two-stroke supercharged diesel!

The Seven-Ups

US, 1973, 103mins, colour

Dir: Philip D'Antoni

Clearly inspired by *The French Connection*, *The Seven-Ups* featured Roy Schneider (Popeye Doyle's sidekick in the earlier film) and a serviceable and fairly violent car chase. Look out for Bill Hickman driving the bad guys' Chevrolet Caprice.

McQ

US, 1974, 111min, colour

Dir: John Sturges

Sturges – remembered for *Bad Day at Black Rock*, *Gunfight at the OK Corral*, *The Magnificent Seven* and *The Great Escape* – directed John Wayne in this violent thriller which was an obvious retort to the success of *Dirty Harry*: right-wing cop with rancid private life does it his way, hands in his badge frequently and shoots everything that moves.

The highlight is a chase, cast in the *Bullitt* mould. Wayne squeezes himself into a green bull-nosed Camaro and pursues the felons in a laundry truck around the Seattle ring road. Later a pair of Mack rigs cube the car – with Wayne cowering in the footwells – by ramming either end down a back alley.

A Buick LeSabre and Ford LTD finish the film with a brutal example of beach rage.

Left top: A 3-litre Vanden Plas Austin being rammed by the Jaguar in *Villain*. A great scene for banger racers. (*Photo: EMI/BFI Stills, Posters and Designs*)

Left centre: Barry Newman's Ford Torino making a mess of some vegetables in *Fear is the Key*. (*Photo: EMI/KLK/Pictorial Press Limited*)

Left bottom: A still from *The Seven-Ups*. The stiff in the boot of the Chevrolet Caprice later turned up as Cliff Barnes in the TV Series *Dallas*. Allegedly he had by that time come back to life. (*Photo: TCF/Pictorial Press Limited*)

Below: Richard Burton assessing the damage done in a used car lot in *Villain*. Just look at all that claret on the Mk2. (*Photo: EMI/BFI Stills, Posters and Designs*)

Seventy three year old John Wayne standing on a skip into which he has just crashed a Ford Capri after jumping Tower Bridge in *Brannigan*. *(Photo: UA/Wallbone/Pictorial Press Limited)*

Opposite top: Comedy carburettor trouble from a Peugeot 504 in *The Pink Panther Strikes Again*. *(Photo: Universal Artists/Pictorial Press Limited)*

Opposite bottom: Dennis Waterman apprehending a villain with the regulation getaway Jag in the backgound in *Sweeney!* *(Photo: Euston Films, BFI Stills, Posters and Designs)*

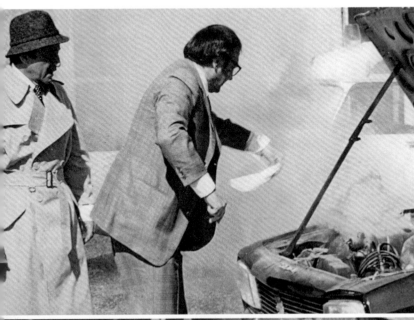

Brannigan

GB, 1975, 111mins, colour

Dir: Douglas Hickox

Hickox gives mid-1970s London a curiously '50s feel in this watchable vehicle for John Wayne (by this time well into his 70s, fully wigged-up and probably not feeling too good – he died two years later of cancer). He takes us around the tourist traps as the action unfolds in a sunny capital of bobbies, barrow boys and red telephone boxes. Wayne is chauffeured by Judy Geeson in a MkI Granada, but the highlight of the film is the car chase. James Booth makes a getaway in a golden sand S-type Jaguar with Wayne in hot pursuit in a yellow 1.6 MkII Capri commandeered from its owner who sits petrified beside him. The climax comes when the Jag leaps a partially raised Tower Bridge while Wayne's Capri flounders in a conveniently placed skip – Ford's best bit of product placement since *Carry on Cabby*. A black 2+2 E-Type features heavily – driven by a hit man out to kill Wayne – but ends in the Thames.

The Pink Panther Strikes Again

GB, 1976, 103mins, colour

Dir: Blake Edwards

This boring sequel to the over-rated 1963 film starred Sellers's most annoying character but featured some glamorous cars and cameos from the likes of Leonard Rossiter in a Triumph 2.5 Pi Mk2. The cartoon series was much more enjoyable than any of the live action *Pink Panther* films.

Sweeney!

GB, 1976, 89mins, colour

Dir: David Wickes

The Sweeney, made by Euston Films for Thames Television, was easily one of the best crime series of the '70s. At the heart of its appeal were convincing car chases through a mucky-looking London that had long since cast-off its 'swinging' credentials. John Thaw, still only in his early 30s but looking much older, added hard-bitten charisma, with Dennis Waterman as his more up-beat sidekick. This spin-off film was a story of political blackmail but opens with a thwarted heist sequence that almost seems like a parody of the TV series, by this time running for three years with high ratings. There is the inevitable Jag getaway car (maroon XJ6 4.2 S1) and a rather unlikely white Lancia Flavia saloon with a roof rack – the same car appears in *Brannigan* waiting on Tower Bridge when the Capri makes the jump. Thaw and co. tool around London in a Mk1 Consul GT (basic spec, big engine with manual shift), and lots of other 1970s British cars feature. *Sweeney 2* was less convincing and the clean-lined MkII Granadas didn't have the same cachet. Language was too clean as well.

Driver

US, 1978, 91mins, colour
Dir: Walter Hill

One critic described *Driver* as 'comic book cops and robbers existentialism' and it is indeed a film stripped down to its bare essentials. The film starts with a 15-minute car chase with no dialogue. Ryan O'Neal is 'The Driver' who, like the rest of the cast, doesn't have a name. He only delivers 350 words of dialogue throughout, with a single deadpan facial expression. Bruce Dern is 'The Detective' who is obsessed with capturing O'Neal because, er, he's never been caught. So he sets up a bank job to lure him, unsuccessfully as it turns out.

The most memorable part of the film, which seems to be shot mostly at night, is the sequence in the underground car park. A gang wants to test O'Neal's skills in a stolen Mercedes 280SE which, although there is no badge on the boot lid, must be a 4.5 V8 (only sold on the American market) if the exhaust note is anything to go by. Slamming the column shift into drive O'Neal performs a series of expert spins and slides that take the perfect orange bodywork of the Mercedes within inches of the car park pillars, whilst throughout the exercise the engine's bellow resonates off the concrete walls. His interviewers seem impressed but 'The Driver' isn't quite finished. He then proceeds to take the Mercedes apart, starting delicately

with just a bumper then clipping fire hydrants, reversing into walls at full throttle, smearing the car down the sides of pillars and tearing off the door before driving into the back of a truck to flatten the roof by a few inches. Never does his expression change.

Later there is a more conventional but definitely superior chase involving a Pontiac Firebird and 'The Driver' behind the wheel of a Chevrolet pick-up truck. The protagonists find themselves in a warehouse where the Firebird ends up in a pit. Sharp viewers will notice the cache of unsold American specification Peugeot 604s.

The London Connection
(aka The Omega Connection)

GB/US, 1979, 100mins, colour
Dir: Robert Clouse

In that depressing age just before the rise of the home VCR, when surviving cinemas offered the temptations of no heating, suspicious hot dogs and 1965 commercials for your local Chinese restaurant, a Disney film was still an event. From the early 1950s Disney had made films on location in the UK, the best being 1963's *The Horse Without a Head*. Sadly this was not a proto-*Godfather* epic but a French-set children v. gangsters movie, however it made good use of Lee Montague, Leo McKern and the 403 Berlina from every other episode of *The Saint*. By the 1970s, British-based Disney films tended towards the sassy (i.e. obnoxious): US hero/heroine visiting an England portrayed in the style of a British Transport film travelogue circa 1954 – a scenario Disney might well have developed into a *Wicker Man* conclusion. But they never did. Spoilsports.

So, we find all-American student (a mature one at that) Luther Sterling (Jeffrey Byron) and his pal Roger Pike (Larry Cedar) right here in London, England. It is very important to emphasise this fact lest the US audience confuse it with London, Ontario.

The director Roger Clouse, who also helmed *Enter the Dragon*, is provided with some pretty nifty car chases such as the dash involving MI5 agents Roy Kinnear and David

A publicity poster for *Driver*. *(Photo: TCF/EMI/Pictorial Press Limited)*

Right: Ryan O'Neal in action in the orange Mercedes 280E in *Driver*. *(Photo: TCF/EMI/BFI Stills, Posters and Designs)*

Battley in their Consul 2500L. As the only Consul worth mentioning is the 3000GT, its wrecking isn't too much of a loss and provides the basis for a decent running gag whereby Kinnear blows up a P6 3500S (don't try this at home children), crashes a Minor 1000 and is finally issued with a Daimler Dingo scout car.

The plot revolves around scientist David Kossoff and evil mastermind Nigel Davenport. Luther and Roger narrowly escape from Nigel's minions in their 1935 Morgan – remember, in 1979 the Midget had rubber bumpers, and a three-wheeled Morgan is pretty 'kooky' (this is Disney and our heroes are meant to be 20 years old). Best of all, they use a BSA motorcycle and sidecar to flee from another minion in a red S-type. By this time, the S-type could be bought for pocket money prices in *Exchange & Mart* and it would not be until well into the next decade that the classic car press would take it seriously. But this old Jaguar is even meaner than the sand-coloured 3.8S wrecked every week in *The Sweeney*. For one, it has machine guns fitted behind the horn grilles (it's a late model) and but for the fact that the BSA carried a rocket launcher, Luther would never be able to save the Western world. However, the Met arrive in their 2500s and Luther is recruited by a CIA type. He's probably still working in Latin America right now. *The London Connection* is barely seen on UK terrestrial TV but may surface on the Disney cable/digital channels. It's worth a look for its strange combination of a 1960s Swinging London plot transposed to the late 1970s with 1950s British stereotypes – all of whom manage to act the heroes off the screen.

The Long Good Friday
GB, 1979, 105mins, colour
Dir: John Mackenzie

This film made Bob Hoskins, that well known Cockney from the Home Counties. As the inheritor of the Krays' king of the underworld crown, his East End gang boss Harold Shand drives an early Silver Shadow which, because it looks ever so slightly tatty – sporting rather tacky whitewall tyres –

clearly isn't going to make it into the second reel. Sure enough, it gets blown up by the 'rival gang' that are trying to unsettle the equilibrium that has existed on Shand's turf for the past 10 years. However, Harold still has his rather nice blue Series 2 XJ6 in which to tool around a pre-Thatcher London of shabby boozers and bombsites. His 'posh crumpet', Helen Mirren, drives a silver Pagoda SL (already nearly a decade out of date but much cooler than the then-current model), while in the opening scenes there is a BMW 2500 saloon which the IRA use to transport the body of one of Shand's murdered associates. The final scene is played out in the back seat of the XJ6: Shand is thrown back against the leather, his face registering anger, surprise and finally resignation as he realises his Irish captors (one of them played by future 007, Pierce Brosnan) are probably driving him to his execution.

Ronin
US, 1998, 121mins, colour
Dir: John Frankenheimer

Ronin feels like one long car chase, which is just as well as the film has little else to recommend it unless you happen to like watching Robert De Niro do, er, Robert De Niro. *Ronin* tells the story of a gang of renegades assembled to steal a mysterious aluminium case, the contents of which are never revealed. The chases – which involve, with one glorious exception, modern saloons – are convincing, however. Frankenheimer, whose CV includes *Grand Prix*, hit on the idea of using British right-hand-drive cars and setting up fake steering wheels for the actors to hold. So when you see a rather worried Mr De Niro driving the Peugeot 406 it is actually the stunt driver alongside who is weaving the car through Parisian underpasses on the tail of a power-sliding BMW M5. Frankenheimer wanted to shoot the chases live so that the cars looked as if they were going as fast as they actually were. To get the required speed, racing drivers were hired: Claude Laginez and Michel Neugarten, who shared the GT2 class-winning 911 that came ninth overall at Le Mans in '97, and ex-Formula I driver Jean-Pierre Jarrier.

Ronin was shot in just days on location in France at a time of year when the light was thin, and gone by 5pm. No red cars were used. One of the techniques employed by Frankenheimer and Robert Fraisse, director of photography, was to shoot on long lenses and get up to 20 seconds of continuous action as the cars approached.

An Audi S8, not even announced when the film was being made, is used to excellent effect. But the best chase unfolds around Nice and the hills, when the felons emerge driving a 25-year-old Mercedes 450SEL 6.9 in a flurry of tyre smoke. There are glorious shots of the M5 power-sliding between kerbs and De Niro's 406 pulls off a couple of exceptionally precise handbrake turns as the action goes on, unrelentingly. 'If I'm going to do a car chase,' said Frankenheimer at the time, 'I'm going to do one that's going to make somebody think about whether or not they want to do another.'

The British Second-Feature

The British B-film is the Cinderella of cinema studies. These humble one-hour epics were designed to be an integral part of a four-hour cinema programme along with the A-film and the Movietone Newsreel ('The Governor stated that independence is not feasible at this time,' Leslie Mitchell usually intoned). Exhibitors could, therefore, sell more confectionery, which in turn the disgruntled patrons could hurl at the screen (and disgruntled many of them were on catching sight of the 'Butchers Film Service' or 'Danziger Brothers' logo). By the end of the 1960s the supporting feature was a largely moribund art form, the one-hour ITV films having assumed their role.

About 70–80% of the B-epics were black and white crime dramas and it is these that surface in the early hours, a reminder of a gentler age when the police would ring their gongs in a deserted street to helpfully alert the baddies to their presence. Choice examples are:

The Hi-Jackers 1963 (aka 'The one with Tony Blair's father-in-law'). Honest haulier Anthony Booth defeats ruthless gangster Derek Francis in his white Mk2 Jaguar. By way of a change, the police use PB Veloxes and FB Victors.

Smokescreen 1964. A blazing Minx MkVII drophead hurtles over the Brighton cliffs in one of the better pieces, boasting a witty lead performance by Peter Vaughn and even a modicum of pathos.

Pit of Darkness 1961. Actually aimed at the lower half of a double bill as opposed to a B-movie proper, but *Pit* is British second-feature through and through. Honest Minx 1600-driving businessman William Franklyn is drugged by ruthless villain Michael Balfour (white tie and black shirt). Mr Balfour favours a 180 Ponton ('it goes like a rocket') but the film's budget is so low that Joe Wadham appears sans Wolseley. Incidentally, Anthony Booth and Nannette Newman did it.

Danger by My Side 1962. The epitome of the B-movie's awful charm, with its Soho nightclub setting (containing about 10 extras) and off-key theme music. Bill Nagy, one of a number of British-based Canadian B-movie leading men, takes part in a daring bullion heist in Croydon High Street. The gang's 1952 MkVII mounts the pavement and, as the stuntmen try to give Oscar-winning performances as Stuntmen Overcome By Ammonia, the hoods flee in an A55 Farina. All except for Bill, of course, who runs into a Belisha beacon. Post prison, Bill has an undercover CID officer assassinated via running him over with a MkI Zephyr-Six travelling at approximately 5mph.

spies & espionage

kiss-kiss, bang-bang, vroom vroom

Timothy Dalton in the Aston V8
Vantage escaping some formidable
pursuers in *The Living Daylights*.
*(Photo: MGM-UA/EON/Pictorial Press
Limited)*

MOST OF THE BEST SPY FILMS were centred on Cold War Europe. There are obviously a few exceptions to this argument – Rank's 1956 Paris-set *The House of Secrets* with Brylcreemed Michael Craig and a good many Traction Avants, or HUAC-inspired drivel such as *I Was a Communist For The FBI*, filled with granite-jawed Federal Agents in 1951 Fords – but my preferences lie with films such as *The Man Between*, with dark Hansa 2400s and Mercedes-Benz 170s lurching through the snow. Few British or American cars could lurch with such élan (although the Phase 1 Standard Vanguard might give them a run for their money).

In fact there are three aspects to the espionage thriller, as established by early post-war spy films that especially appeal to car enthusiasts. The first, as seen in the 1961 Billy Wilder film *One Two Three!*, is the curiosity value of Warsaw Pact cars to a Western audience. In Wilder's comedy the KGB's Moskvitch 407 is rudely compared to a '1938 Nash' and literally falls to pieces in pursuit of James Cagney's 'Adenauer' Mercedes 300c. By the 1960s, *Funeral in Berlin* could boast not only a DDR Police EMW 340 but also its 1956 replacement, the 2.4-litre IFA saloon that serves as Colonel Stok's official car and looks very much like a Phase II Vanguard. Meanwhile, on the other side of the Berlin Wall, the NSU Ro80 was less than two years from launch.

The second aspect of a good spy film is encapsulated by the black Mercedes 300c that serves as Cagney's official car in *One Two Three!* The viewer can almost chart the progression of West Germany's economic re-birth through the changing sequence of cars, all of them seemingly sporting a white steering wheel – Borgward Isabellas, BMW 'Baroque Angels' and especially the varieties of Mercedes-Benz. From the solid 180D Ponton taxis to the vast 300 limousines, a 1950s or '60s M-B implies indestructibility and purpose. Even if the 300ds that grace 1965's *The Quiller Memorandum* are but a few years old, they are undeniably impressive in their Teutonic manner, but it is their successor that became the only car for any self-respecting super villain. The 1966 Franco-German film *The Defector* featured

Montgomery Clift in his final screen role but it also starred a Mercedes-Benz 600. By 1969, the 600 was becoming the ideal vehicle from which to rule certain nations and one formed part of Ernst Blofeld's fleet in *On Her Majesty's Secret Service* – spy film accolades come no higher.

Mentioning *OHMSS* returns us to the 007 series, but these are dealt with separately, if only in the belief that there can be very very few readers who are unaware of the DB5, the Esprit, the 2CV *et al*. The other spy films produced at the height of 'Bond mania' – *circa* 1964–66 – are either slavish imitators or the deliberate antithesis of the genre, and in either case provide an excellent array of cars. For Jaguar fans there is George Nader as super agent Jerry Cotton in his red 4.2 E-type coupé, star of many a West German *krimimovie* plus Italy's *Diabolik* with his matching black and white E-types. Of course, to make a film in the true 007 spirit, a fair sized budget is essential for that air of international glamour, otherwise the epic will resemble the *Man From Uncle* spin-off, *The Spy In The Green Hat*, and boast a Rambler Marlin. At least it lurches in the best Hansa 2400 fashion. Alternatively, there are the 1960s adaptations of Len Deighton and John le Carré that continue the ethos of *The Third Man* into the 1960s. Younger viewers of *The Ipcress File* may be startled to see how distant mid-1960s London now appears, with Special Branch driving Austin A99s and trilby hats aplenty.

But for sheer, unremitting gloom reminiscent of Graham Greene, one cannot surpass Richard Burton and Claire Bloom heading towards the Berlin Wall in a Moskvitch in *The Spy Who Came In From The Cold*, or *The Deadly Affair* with a weary James Mason pursuing a dilapidated MG Magnette ZB in his A55 Farina through a rainswept unswinging London. But one of the finest, most suspenseful and plausible car chases in any spy film occurs in *Callan*, a low-budget 1974 British adaptation of an ITV series, which boasts only a white Range Rover and a black 1968 Jaguar S-type. As in any genre of film, cinematic ingenuity does count for more than budget.

Dr No

GB, 1962, 105mins, colour
Dir: Terence Young

The formula established by the first of the 007 films is deceptively simple – cast up-and-coming young leading man Sean Connery and make the character of Bond an upper-class romantic, add a soupçon of Joe Lampton-brand label snobbery, and make your hero a government-licensed cad, defending Queen and Commonwealth. Add colour cinematography, overseas locations and dubbed beautiful ladies and you have a box-office hit for those 'Wind of Change' years as Commander Bond issues advice to the CIA's Felix Leiter (a pre-hairspray Jack Lord) and orders to his local contact 'Quarrell'. In fact, the racial undercurrent of Dr No now makes for rather uneasy viewing.

Much of the automotive interest of Dr No is from the cars in pre-independence Jamaica – an assortment of 1950s Chevrolets and Ford 105E Anglias. The police use black Mk2 Consuls, villains drive old Cadillacs and Bond pilots a Mk2 Sunbeam Alpine – at least it's more exciting than the novel's Hillman Minx. However, a keynote is struck by Anthony Dawson's PA Velox, establishing a 007 film adage: 'Doomed inadequate villainous sidekicks will display their ineptitude by driving mundane cars.'

From Russia with Love

GB, 1963, 110mins, colour
Dir: Terence Young

This has the finest quartet of villainy – Walter Gotell, Lotte Lenya, Valdek Sheyball and the great Robert Shaw – the best loyal ally, Pedro Armendariz, and a much more relaxed performance by Mr C, who also seemed to have toned down the rather odd Boston-Irish accent present in Dr No. This is the only film to feature 007's favoured Bentley but the automotive highlights are to be found in Istanbul, where fans of 1950s Yank tanks and six-cylinder Opel Kapitans will have a field day. Armendariz displays his Anglo-American loyalties by using a Ford Galaxie station wagon and a Rolls-Royce Silver Wraith, whilst the Bulgarian embassy is clearly on an economy drive as they are reduced to using a down-at-heel Onze Normale. Had they shown more initiative, they could have borrowed a Tatra from the Czech embassy, but at least their staff cars weren't Russian-built – it's difficult to shadow a top secret agent when you're driving a Pobeda.

Goldfinger

GB, 1964, 105mins, colour
Dir: Guy Hamilton

Cinematic stardom is often in inverse ratio to actual screentime so before discussing the Aston Martin DB5, we should note that its part in the film is brief and that there are several other vehicles of note – Goldfinger's gold Rolls-Royce, the black Lincoln Continental destined for the crusher and the Red Peril in their fleet of 180 Pontons – establishing another rule of Bond: 'Whilst occidental henchmen and stunt drivers grimace, oriental henchmen gesticulate.'

Nevertheless, the Aston Martin made the film. It was of an acceptable marque (unlike the parvenu E-type), it boasted rakish styling (unlike the Alvis TE21, Daimler Dart or Jensen CV8), it was luxurious (definitely unlike the big Healey) and it had an aggressive macho image (unlike the Bentley Contintental or the Bristol 407).

It boosted Aston Martin's sales too and would become a kind of Bond visual shorthand that featured in many spy spoof films of the era. Four real-life Bond DB5s were made, two film vehicles and two promotional vehicles, all now in private hands.

Thunderball

GB, 1965, 125mins, colour
Dir: Terence Young

The first Bond film where the length begins to seem interminable – not helped by the endless underwater travelogue sequences. The DB5 makes a guest appearance, but there's little else of automotive interest – Morris Minor convertible, Ford Mustang and Triumph Herald 1200 drophead – see the Dr No rule for inadequate sidekicks.

Sean Connery with his Aston Martin in *Goldfinger* on location in Switzerland. *(Photo: UA/EON/Pictorial Press Limited)*

The iconic DB5 in *Goldfinger* was the inspiriation for Corgi's greatest model. *(Photo: UA/EON/Pictorial Press Limited)*

BMT 216A

The Toyota 2000GT used by Bond in *You Only Live Twice*. (Photo: UA/EON/Pictorial Press Limited)

Pursuing villains get their come-uppance in the snow in *On Her Majesty's Secret Service*. (Photo: UA/EON/Pictorial Press Limited)

The famous two-wheel stunt in *Diamonds Are Forever*. Spot the deliberate mistake. (Photo: UA/EON/Pictorial Press Limited)

You Only Live Twice

GB, 1967, 111mins, colour
Dir: Lewis Gilbert

Superb John Barry theme song, as interpreted by Nancy Sinatra, the most beautiful actresses in the history of Japanese cinema and, for fans of chintzmobiles, the Tokyo scenes will be indispensable. 007's Toyota 2000GT is a reminder that by 1966 the Japanese Motor Industry had overtaken that of the UK. Naturally, the villainous henchmen in their Crown De-Luxe gesticulate rather a lot. The convertible 2000GT was specially built because Connery was too big to fit into the Coupé model and there were filming difficulties because of the lack of interior space. The convertible now sits in the Toyota museum in Japan.

On Her Majesty's Secret Service

GB, 1969, 127mins, colour
Dir: Peter Hunt

George Lazenby gives a pretty assured performance for a non-professional actor, and his manly blubbing at the conclusion is almost of the Michael Caine/Jack Hawkins calibre. In this low-key Bond, only the Mercedes-Benz 600, Aston Martin DBS and Mercury Cougar really stand out.

Diamonds Are Forever

GB, 1971, 114mins, colour
Dir: Guy Hamilton

The third-generation Mustang Mach 1 perfectly encapsulates the central malaise of the film; both being bloated middle-aged parodies of an early 1960s idea. However, despite the fact that Sean Connery's performance now has as much conviction as his toupee, all is not lost since the film features Charles Gray – probably Bournemouth's most terrifying ex-estate agent – as Blofeld plus a cameo by an H-plate Triumph Stag. This is a sad reminder of the days when the young BLMC empire hoped to produce a rival to the Mercedes-Benz SL, although the Stag is possibly better placed in a Bond film than in *Dracula AD 1972*.

Live and Let Die

GB, 1973, 116mins, colour
Dir: Guy Hamilton

Yes, it stars Roger Moore, but he is quite acceptable in his David Niven-like manner, and at least Roger is a better choice for Commander Bond than Burt Reynolds is. Furthermore, he sports a much better haircut than in *The Persuaders* and looks pretty groovy in a safari suit. That said, the

Airport mayhem in *Live and Let Die*.
(Photo: UA/EON/Pictorial Press Limited)

The Lotus Esprit submarine in *The Spy Who Loved Me* is filmed underwater by Larmar Boren and crew. *(Photo: UA/EON/Pictorial Press Limited)*

The Mercedes 280S on track in *Octopussy*. No, that's not Roger on the roof. *(Photo: UA/EON/Pictorial Press Limited)*

blacksploitation theme smacks of desperation – the early Connery Bonds created rather than followed trends – the talents of Yaphett Kotto are totally wasted and the voodoo sequences seem to be aimed at devotees of *Love Thy Neighbour.* There is little of motoring interest, but the police cars in the speedboat sequence do emphasise the elephantine size of pre-fuel-crisis American cars, whilst the double-decker bus pursuit could herald a new crossover for British cinema – 007 Meets *Summer Holiday* (Jane Seymour does sound awfully like Una Stubbs)…

The Man With the Golden Gun
GB, 1974, 119mins, colour
Dir: Guy Hamilton

Probably Roger's best 007 performance, together with *The Spy Who Loved Me*, and Christopher Lee's master-villain is certainly the most charismatic since Donald Pleasence. Sadly, the film attempts to ride another 1970s bandwagon, that of the HK Kung Fu epic, and the theme song is dire. There is, though, slightly more of interest for car enthusiasts – the array of Japanese chintzmobiles in Bangkok and Hong Kong are particularly impressive – although the choice of AMC's not very charismatic Hornet X as the car plane is as unfortunate as the 'comedy' music that accompanies the stuntwork. N.B. Beware the *Carry On at Your Convenience* dialogue.

The Spy Who Loved Me
GB, 1977, 120mins, colour
Dir: Lewis Gilbert

A jolly theme song, plus Roger's assured Niven-style light comedy touch makes this my favourite Moore-Bond. Then, of course, there is the Lotus Esprit, the basis for Dinky's last really good die-cast model, and definitely a world apart from the Renault 16-engined Europa.

Actually, the best Lotus sequence is not the sub-aqua battle but the chase between Roger and Jaws, the latter in a black MkIV Cortina/Taunus. Not only do the villains grimace in the best stuntman/walk-on fashion but also any astute viewer would realise the inevitability of the Cortina crashing.

Henchmen to a top international criminal should run a Granada 3000S at the very least. The other featured vehicle of note is the Leyland Sherpa belonging to the Cairo Electricity Board, although why they should run a right-hand-drive van with English script on the panels remains a mystery.

Moonraker
GB, 1979, 121mins, colour
Dir: Lewis Gilbert

An interminably boring film, with Roger's performance heralding a steady decline into tired self-parody, and hardly any cars of note aside from a pre-war Rolls-Royce. Meanwhile, Michel Lonsdale portrays super-villain Hugo Drax with the despondent air of a French actor with Welles and Trauffaut on his CV who has landed yet another bad English-language role.

For Your Eyes Only
GB, 1981, 122mins, colour
Dir: John Glen

Aka *The One With the 2CV.* A 007 film of little automotive interest aside from the Spanish sequences of the yellow deux-chevaux being pursued by black Peugeot 504s. Playing Bond 'straight' doesn't have to equate with bland – see *From Russia with Love* – and during the film's longueurs, the viewer tends to think fondly of Dean Martin as Matt Helm.

Octopussy
GB, 1983, 125mins, colour
Dir: John Glen

Demented General Steven Berkoff drives a 1968 Mercedes-Benz 280S along a railway line and is shot by Walter Gotell for mutiny, rampant over-acting and wrecking the only decent car in the Russian Army. The Indian sequences contain the usual stock footage of Hindustani Ambassadors and Premier Padminis, combined with very obvious Pinewood sets, but Roger is such a game old chap that one hardly likes to criticise.

A View to a Kill

GB, 1985, 125mins, colour
Dir: John Glen

Oh dear. Roger's performance as a secret agent is now as convincing as Charles Hawtrey in *Carry On Spying* – a far cry from the heady days of *The Man Who Haunted Himself* and *Vendetta for a Saint*. Then there is that bisected Renault 11, proof that the lessons of *The Man With the Golden Gun* went unheeded – however ingenious the stuntwork, a deeply boring car will remain a deeply boring car. You could halve, quarter or purée a Renault 11 without diluting its anodyne qualities. Still, there is a Silver Cloud in the Ascot footage and a guest appearance by Patrick Macnee to remind viewers of the unforgettable Moore/Macnee portrayals of Holmes and Watson in *Sherlock Holmes in New York*.

The Living Daylights

GB, 1987, 125mins, colour
Dir: John Glen

It is oft forgotten how po-faced many 1980s films really were. Timothy Dalton certainly looks macho enough in his Aston Martin DBS V8, but the entire exercise is so humourless. Where's the glossy cinematography, the heavily-mascaraed femme fatales and the sun-shaded light-suited extras driving a flotilla of black Tatras?

Licence to Kill

US, 1989, 126mins, colour
Dir: John Glen

Any 007 film where Bond is rude and aggressive to Q does not deserve a place in this book.

Consumerist wish fulfilment with US and 'British' marques in *Die Another Day*. (Photo: UA/EON)

GoldenEye

GB/US, 1995, 124mins, colour
Dir: Martin Campbell

A film with the perfect 007-wagon compromise for the 1990s – an Aston Martin DB5 for Sunday best (heritage Britain *et al*) and a BMW 23 Roadster for everyday wear. For these reasons the film initially ran into some British tabloid flak, but given that by 1994 the world's fourth largest motor manufacturer had just become a loss-making subsidiary of BMW …

Tomorrow Never Dies

US/GB, 1997, 114mins, colour
Dir: Roger Spottiswoode

If a film really has to be a two-hour commercial for the BMW 750i, at least ensure that it is as entertaining as this 007 effort.

The World is Not Enough

GB/US, 1999, 128 mins, colour
Dir: Michael Apted

A lacklustre villain is balanced with some jolly sequences of a radio-controlled BMW 750L careering around a car park. All good spy films should have a car park sequence.

Die Another Day

GB/US, 2002, 120mins, colour
Dir: Lee Tamahori

Although Bond's newest mission starts with a spectacular hovercraft chase through a minefield in Korea, he gets to drive an Aston Martin Vanquish through a palace built of ice. The villain motors about in a 400bhp Jaguar XKR convertible and the bimbo favours a Ford Thunderbird.

Topkapi

US, 1964, 119mins, colour
Dir: Jules Dassin

There was a moment in the early 1960s when the Lincoln Continental was the only American car to be seen in. Peter Ustinov looks strangely reluctant here, however – perhaps recalling the fate of JFK as he rode his long-wheelbase version through Dallas. *Topkapi*, from a novel by Eric Ambler, was an international crime caper about thieves trying to rob an Istanbul museum. Ustinov's 'Arthur' drives the getaway car for the promise of a Rolls-Royce.

The Ipcress File

GB, 1965, 109mins, colour
Dir: Sidney J. Furie

Although Michael Caine's first major role was in *Zulu*, Harry Palmer was the part that forged his reputation. The Len Deighton character was seen by Harry Saltzman as an antidote to James Bond, and Caine's working-class, Mozart-loving gourmet in mackintosh and heavy spectacle frames still serves a welcome dose of reality. He lives in Notting Hill, and doesn't even own a car. A partially alienated organisation man able to mitigate, but never fully overcome, the effects of his superiors' arrogance and opportunism, Palmer seems more compelling than ever after 40 years in which Bond has saved the world for democracy by ever more lavish means. Caine had three more outings as Palmer – *Funeral in Berlin*, *Billion Dollar Brain* and the almost posthumous *Bullet to Beijing*.

Instead of a private Bentley or personalised Aston, Palmer drives a MkIII Zodiac pool car, investigating a case of disappearing scientists. For two scenes, when he thinks he has tracked them down, Palmer uses Gordon Jackson's Mk2 Jag. The villains escape and it's back to the Zodiac, and in a key moment Jackson is assassinated behind its wheel. The use of the traffic lights in the scene is typical of Sydney J. Furie's direction. Furie directed *The Young Ones* two years later (whatever you think of Cliff Richard, that film's visual composition is superb). In *Ipcress* the

trademark double-decker confirms that Palmer is in London after escaping the villains' hideout (supposedly in Albania). The scene in the underground car park with the Mercedes fintail ambulance is memorable, but the only significant vehicle is an elderly Bentley Continental driven by the villain.

Funeral in Berlin features another outdated symbol of luxury and power, a 1960 Cadillac Eldorado convertible in gold, and lovers of East European machinery will enjoy the EMW police car that whisks Palmer away to an interview with the Russian Colonel who wants to defect to the west, played by Oscar Homolka. The intriguing saloon Homolka uses as official transport is an IFA P240, East Germany's most prestigious vehicle. *Billion Dollar Brain*, directed by Ken Russell, has much less to recommend it apart from a Coleman Milne Ford Zodiac limousine; although there's some good footage of a red Mk2 Cortina slithering about on the frozen lakes of Finland.

Our Man Flint

US, 1965, 108mins, colour
Dir: Daniel Mann

Played by James Coburn with relish and straight-faced poise, Flint was perhaps the best Bond spoof, a freelance secret agent of limitless charm and sophisticated tastes, so multilingual as to be able to converse with dolphins. His main client was Lloyd Kramden (Lee J. Cobb) of ZOWIE (the Zonal Organization for World Intelligence and Espionage). As an American agent, Flint had to drive an American sports car so we briefly see him, with his multipurpose gun/cigarette lighter, behind the wheel of an Excalibur. Clearly this Corvette-based Mercedes SSK pastiche wasn't quite so laughable in those days: in the '70s it tended to be driven by successful porn stars. The sequel, *In like Flint* (1967) failed to recapture the charm of the original. Flint uncovers a female spy ring that has kidnapped the president, but all the women look plastic, the sets look like, well, sets and it turns into a film few could sit through even in the name of irony. And you don't even get to see the Excalibur.

Top left: Peter Ustinov's awful English ex-pat 'Arthur' uses a feather duster on the Lincoln Continental in *Topkapi*. *(Photo: UA/Filmways/Pictorial Press Limited)*

Top right: James Coburn in a clinch with a girl at a drive-in movie in *Our Man Flint*. The car is a Sunbeam Alpine. *(Photo: TCF/Pictorial Press Limited)*

Right: Michael Caine with Sten gun in *The Ipcress File*. The ambulance is a once-common Ford Thames. *(Photo: Rank/BFI Collections)*

Top left: The 'doomed-from-the-start' Fiat 1400 in *Deadlier than the Male*. (Photo: Rank/Pictorial Press Limited)

Top right: Dean Martin as Matt Helm getting in a mess in the back of his converted Ford Station Wagon in *The Silencers*. (Photo: Columbia/BFI Collections)

Bottom: George Segal having removed a bomb from beneath his Mercedes 190SL in *The Quiller Memorandum*. (Photo: Rank/Pictorial Press Limited)

Deadlier than the Male

GB, 1966, 101mins, colour

Dir: Ralph Thomas

This Fiat 1400 Sedan is a classic case of what cars-in-film spotters know as the 'doomed-from-first-moment-on-screen vehicle'. Much the same could be said of the film itself, a lame attempt to resuscitate the 'Bulldog' Drummond character in the '60s Bond idiom.

The Defector

Fr/W Ger 1966, 101mins, colour

Dir: Raoul Lévy

The 1966 Cold War plodder was the last thing Montgomery Clift did. In a sense, the most influential car on this was the Chevrolet Bel Air in which Clift was badly injured a few years before, costing him the extraordinary good looks and intensity of his early performances. It was when returning from a dinner party at Elizabeth Taylor's house that he lost control of his Chevrolet on a dangerous curve and hit a telegraph pole. Taylor saved his life.

Here he drives an early Porsche 911 and the final scenes feature a Mercedes 600 – probably on loan from Mercedes if the number plates are anything to go by. Also, if you are quick with the freeze-frame there is an exquisite moment for Mercedes anoraks – a 300SE Cabriolet in orange with a prototype full-width SL-type grille that just happened to be passing when the cameras were rolling. The car never saw the light of day. This is one of the earliest appearances of a Mercedes 600 on screen, although it was always a villain's car in the Bond films: nothing else had quite the same feeling of power and menace.

The Silencers
(Matt Helm series)

US, 1966, 103mins, colour

Dir: Phil Karlson

In a series of spy novels written by American Donald Hamilton between 1960 and 1993 Matt Helm is a hard-boiled private eye in the mould of Mickey Spillane's Mike Hammer. Producer Irving Allen used Hamilton's books as the basis for a spy spoof starring Dean Martin, having ended his partnership with Albert R. Broccoli because he felt the Bond novels were 'worthless'.

Martin nudges and winks his way through all four films in the series. *The Silencers* features a Ford station wagon with rear seats removed to make space for a button-operated shag palace in true '60s style, though the most notable car in the series is a Rolls-Royce Silver Cloud which, by way of camouflage, transforms itself into an advertising hoarding.

Fans of the books take Helm very seriously and hate the films which, though initially glossy and seductive, are actually quite difficult to sit through. Dean Martin was far too boozed to convince as a super spy and all the sets look a bit wobbly. The station wagon, which has its own bar, features in a chase sequence with a bogus Police car fitted with bull-bars.

The Quiller Memorandum

GB, 1966, 105mins, colour

Dir: Michael Anderson

In a Harold Pinter script that keeps little more than names and a plot premise from Adam Hall's novel *The Berlin Memorandum*, George Segal plays an American agent brought in to work under Alec Guinness in the search for neo-Nazis in Berlin. The city's architecture is used brilliantly, as Nazi monuments like the Olympic Stadium of 1936 contrast with new structures that promise a modernist ideal of the late-century social-democratic metropolis. New concrete freeways and flyovers are another part of the Utopian civic vision, and driving and chase sequences feature prominently. Segal is given an early red Porsche 911, and escapes in the film's climax by destroying a Mercedes SL with the bomb that the Nazis have set to kill him. Unusually, the screenplay specified the cars that each character would drive – including the year and model of several Mercedes. Pinter himself had just purchased a specially modified SE cabriolet from Stuttgart – a car he was to keep in mint condition until it was stolen in the 1980s.

Crossplot

GB, 1969, 97mins, colour

Dir: Alvin Rakoff

With its TV production values and dodgy back-projection, this little bit of nonsense looks much older than it is, despite the fact that Roger Moore has started brushing his hair forward and wearing high button suits (he was already 42 by this time though he didn't look it). Post *The Saint*, he has swapped his P1800 Volvo for a much more hip Alfa Romeo 1750 Spider (Duetto round-tail), and the cars are the film's salvation. Moore's a work hard, play hard kind of guy: staying up all night smooching young ladies (half his age probably) in his Park Lane flat, gunning the Alfa to his job in the city still dressed in his monkey suit from the night before, grabbing a pint of milk off a float (but remembering to pay for it) and screeching into an underground car park where Michael Robbins (Olive's Husband in *On the Buses*) is the peerlessly sneering attendant. Later the Alfa is used as a prop in an advertising shoot, despite the fact that just a few minutes earlier Moore had crashed it into a shop window while under the influence of pot. Alexis Kanner plays a hippie aristocrat who drives an Opus-HRF (I think) glass fibre retro-roadster which we are expected to believe is a real veteran car. Other four-wheel stars are an S1 Bentley (the baddies including Francis Matthews, the voice of *Captain Scarlet*) and a Phantom V, probably Lew Grade's own car. The producers must have done a deal with Ford as every police car and random vehicle encountered in the chase is a MkIV Zephyr.

Callan

GB, 1974, 106mins, colour

Dir: Don Sharp

This was a rewrite of the first episode of Edward Woodward's 1967–73 TV series about a lonely, downbeat spy who killed for the government. He hunts down his prey cross-country in a white, two-door Range Rover with dark windows, and Jag-lovers cringe as they see the mint dark blue S-type of war criminal Schneider (Carl Mohner)

smashed by a train when it gets stuck on a level crossing. One of the best low-budget chases in cinema.

S*P*Y*S

US, 1974, 112mins, colour

Dir: Irvin Kershner

The French-plated 2CV was probably meant to endow Donald Sutherland and Elliot Gould with then-fashionable hippy-chic, but the script was inferior to M*A*S*H and the film never really got going. File under 'Avoid'.

Austin Powers
International Man of Mystery

US, 1997, 89mins, colour

Dir: Jay Roach

The series 1 E-type roadster in *Austin Powers, International Man of Mystery* easily out-curves Liz Hurley, who in shame pretends to be reading the gear-lever. Part of the film is a most excellent homage to American studio-bound 'recreations' of England – and British TV espionage heroes like Jason King – and Mike Myers's character has generated two sequels: *The Spy Who Shagged Me* and *Goldmember*.

The Avengers

US, 1998, 89mins, colour

Dir: Jeremiah Chechik

This recreation of a classic British TV series of the '60s did nothing to enhance the reputation of either Ralph Fiennes (Steed) or Uma Thurman (Mrs Peel) and there is very little good that can be said about it, although some might feel it worth watching for the snug catsuit seen here, or perhaps even the E-type Jag, despite the whitewalls.

It's safe to say that *The Avengers* is one of the truly great stinkers of recent years. But it does fairly successfully recapture the sometimes eerie, other-worldly feel of the original TV series which always featured a good selection of cars, everything from Steed's vintage Bentley to Emma Peel's Lotus Elan and Tara King's AC 428 convertible. Unfortunately, the bowler-wearing Fiennes does resemble Stan Laurel.

Right: The retro roadster with key start used in *Crossplot*. *(Photo: UA/Tribune/Pictorial Press Limited)*

Bottom left: Mike Myers strikes a triumphal pose with Liz Hurley at the wheel of an E-type in *Austin Powers, International Man of Mystery*. *(Photo: Guild/Newline/Copella/KC/Median/Eric's Boy/Pictorial Press Limited)*

Bottom centre: The S-type was at least six years old when *Callan* was released, so its demise was near-inevitable. *(Photo: EMI/Magnum/BFI Stills, Posters and Designs)*

Bottom right: Leather-clad Uma Thurman, with her E-type parked ready in *The Avengers*. *(Photo: Warner/Pictorial Press Limited)*

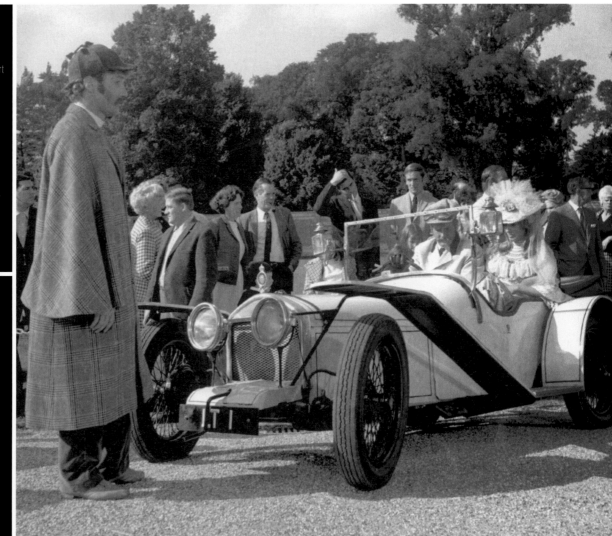

euro-drama

the chrysler 180 of world cinema

THE EURO-DRAMA, with its close stablemates the Euro-Comedy and the Euro-Epic, came of age in the 1960s to strike dread into the hearts of cinemagoers everywhere. The typical Euro-Drama was a cunning combination of American money, Italian studios (Cine-Citta), a French leading man, British character actors and a Spanish location. Actors would speak in their own language before being post-synched and it was not unusual for the actual locale to remain unspecified, leaving the viewer to rely on his/her knowledge of car licence plates. The title incorporated the word 'Affair' or 'Sanction', the name Dino de Laurentis had to appear in the credits and at least one of the leading men sported a hearthrug atop his head. For example:

Operation Amsterdam
UK, 1959, 104mins, b&w
Dir: Michael McCarthy
An unusual entry – a British (Rank) backed Euro-Drama with a sterling cast and a Second World War setting. Four allied agents have stolen Nazi diamonds. Anyway, a film with a Mercedes-Benz 540K cannot be entirely devoid of merit.

The Jerry Cotton series (1965–1969)
West Germany's answer to James Bond, featuring groovy Peter Thomas music and imported American B-actor George Nader in a Guards Red E-type 4.2 coupé.

Diabolik (aka Danger: Diabolik)
It/Fr, 1968, 98mins, colour
Dir: Mario Bava
Mr Diabolik, played by US B-movie lead John Phillip Law, is a swinging international criminal operating out of an anonymous European state (all right, it's really Cine-Citta). John Phillip, head to foot in black leather, drives a white Series 1 E-type coupé, accompanied by a truly groovy theme tune and a first-class support cast (Michel Piccoli, Terry-Thomas). In the credits lurks the name of Dino de Laurentis.

Cold Sweat

Fr/It, 1970, 94mins, colour

Dir: Terence Young

Charles Bronson being macho, although it's not quite right when we find him behind the wheel of a girly Peugeot 204 convertible. Actually a cut above most of this ilk, with a fine high-speed driving sequence along mountain roads in an Opel Commodore GS Coupé – much more his kind of car.

The Burglars

Fr/It ,1971, 120mins, colour

Dir: Henri Verneuil

Boasts Jean-Paul Belmondo, Omar Sharif and a really good car chase across Athens between a 124 Special T, Fiat's own 1600E-beater, and an Opel Admiral, GM-Germany's Viscount equivalent. Apparently Belmondo performed many of his own stunts.

Confessions of a Police Captain
(aka Confessions of a Police Commissioner to the District Attorney)

It, 1972, 101mins, colour

Dir: Damiano Damiani

Martin Balsam is a senior copper driving around Italy in his Giulia 1600 TI rooting out corruption.

The Master Touch
(aka Un uomo da rispettarre)

It/W Ger 1972, 112mins, colour

Dir: Michele Lupo

An Italian film with a Hamburg setting starring a superannuated American. The poster boasts Kirk Douglas (looking the same age as son Michael) able to split a car in half and open a safe with music. Most of the cars featured are late '60s euro boxes – Opels come in for some abuse.

Left: John Phillip Law, girl and white E-type Jaguar strike a pose in *Diabolik*. (Photo: Dino de Laurentis/ BFI Stills, Posters and Designs.)

Below: Part of the car chase in *The Burglars* with the Fiat 124 Special T escaping down a flight of steps. (Photo: Columbia/Vides/Pictorial Press Limited)

CHARLES BRONSON
LE FLINGUEUR

Ste EXPL Ets LALANDE COURBET 91 WISSOUS

The Mechanic

US, 1972, 95mins, colour
Dir: Michael Winner

Charles Bronson plays Arthur Bishop, an emotionless chap who kills people for a living. Still, he does get to drive an Alfa 2600 saloon that, along with a very early Fiat 130 saloon, is destroyed fairly early in the proceedings.

Caravan to Vaccares
(aka Le Passenger)

GB/Fr, 1974, 93mins, colour
Dir: Geoffrey Reeve

Charlotte Rampling was to lend this adaptation of an Alistair Maclean novel some Euro-Class (not a hope) and there's an exploding VW Beetle. And that really is Graham Hill playing the helicopter pilot.

The Marseilles Contract
(aka The Destructors)

GB/Fr, 1974, 87mins, colour
Dir: Robert Parrish

A must for all 504 fans and fanciers of Anthony Quinn in a toupee, James Mason looking woeful and Michael Caine giving his 'Invasion of the Zombies' performance. Good chase sequence features an Alfa Montreal and a Porsche 911 Targa.

Mahogany

US, 1975, 108mins, colour
Dir: Berry Gordy

This vehicle for Diana Ross tells the story of a fashion model and her complex love life, but Italian car fans will wince when the Iso Grifo gets totalled. Fans of good acting will just wince.

Ransom

GB, 1975, 89mins, colour
Dir: Casper Wrede

Sir Sean made some odd choices, such as to play Col. Nils Tahlvik, a Scandinavian military policeman with an Edinburgh accent. The film is leaden but at least the British Ambassador drives a P6 3500.

The Swiss Conspiracy

US/W Ger 1975, 90mins, colour
Dir: Jack Arnold

Two Ferrari Daytona Spiders feature in this dreary tale of intrigue in the world of international banking, along with a Mercedes 600 Pullman and a Fiat 130 saloon.

cars index

Illustrations are shown in italics.

films index

Illustrations are shown in italics. Alternative film titles are in parentheses.